Gael
Lindenfield's
101
Morale
Boosters

Gael Lindenfield's

101 Morale Boosters

Instant comfort for difficult times

piatkus

To Stuart, my husband, whose unfailing support and consistently positive outlook underpins my own morale and has helped me through so many difficult times.

PIATKUS

First published in Great Britain in 2010 by Piatkus

A CIP catalogue record for this book is available from the British Library

The stories and quotes attributed to clients in this book are based on real life experiences. For confidentiality reasons, the names and details of the stories have been altered to disguise the identity of the people concerned.

ISBN 978-0-7499-4293-9

Designed by Goldust Design and typeset by Sam Charrington Design

Printed and bound in Great Britain by Clays Ltd, St Ives Plc

Papers used by Piatkus are natural, renewable and recyclable products sourced from well-managed forests and certified in accordance with the rules of the Forest Stewardship Council.

Mixed Sources
Product group from well-managed forests and other controlled sources
www.fsc.org Cert no. SGS-COC-004081
© 1996 Forest Stewardship Council
FSC

Piatkus
An imprint of
Little, Brown Book Group
100 Victoria Embankment
London EC4Y 0DY

An Hachette UK Company
www.hachette.co.uk
www.piatkus.co.uk

Contents

Acknowledgements

First and foremost, I want to thank the people whose inspirational stories and words I have used in this book. Although the names and the details of your stories have sometimes had to be disguised, you know who you are. I feel privileged to have been witness to your courage as you have gone through your difficult challenges. Thank you so much for sharing your pain and your experiences in order to help the readers of this book.

Thank you also to everyone who has generously contributed their professional expertise. Many of you have opened my eyes to new strategies and approaches which I am so pleased to have been able to share here.

It has been a great pleasure to return to Piatkus for the publication of this book. A big thank you goes to every member of the team that has been involved in this project. Without exception, you have been professionally skilled, always approachable and ever ready to offer help and advice.

Similarly, it has been a joy to continue to work with Jane Graham-Maw, my agent and friend.

Even after twenty-seven years of practice, I still find writing a highly stressful activity. I am not sure that I could ever do it without the support that I receive from my friends and family. I wrote most of this book in my home in Spain, so this time I am especially grateful to my friends in Rota, on the Costa de la Luz of Andalusia. In particular, José and Susana, Janet and Pepe, Grace and Annabelle were amazingly supportive. They frequently supplied me with delicious ready-to-eat meals and would also seduce me away from the computer for breaks that I had forgotten I needed.

Introduction

One spring morning last year my husband and I were sitting in a local restaurant waiting for our daughter to join us for lunch. We were reflecting on how amazing it felt to be able to do this, since three months previously our daughter had decided to 'settle down' after many globe-trotting years and had moved into a beautiful house just walking distance from ours.

Later, as we all sipped our coffee after a happy, relaxing lunch together, we started to talk about the financial crisis in the USA and UK that was then just gathering force. My daughter is a financial lawyer and so I naturally enquired as to how this might affect her. She replied: 'I've been giving it a great deal of thought and, in view of the situation, I think it might be best for me to move back to Asia.'

Instantly, I burst into tears, overwhelmed by utter despair. But within a minute or two, I had recovered my composure and was back to being the supportive mother and positive resilient adult that I truly consider myself to be. I pointed out that this was just another challenge that would, in time, offer us all many positive possibilities. And indeed, my predictions have since been realised. My daughter is now happily working and living in Hong Kong.

We have all learnt how to talk to each other via video links and my husband and I find our trips to Asia both exciting and enlightening.

My ability to deal well with setbacks is a privilege that I will never take for granted. Life can feel literally hell and impossibly daunting without it. I have been lucky in that I had a chance to learn in my early thirties how to deal with these kinds of debilitating emotional reactions to setbacks. And, since then, I have had many opportunities to put them into practice in real life. This is why I was able to regain control so quickly after hearing my daughter's news, whereas the old Gael would have plunged headlong into a spiral of despair.

As I am sure everyone reading this knows, the financial crisis my family discussed that day in the restaurant became global. It triggered a deep recession and a degree of hardship that threw many nations into fear and panic. The psychological knock-on effects on individuals were alarming; statistics showed that depression and anxiety disorders were escalating and the morale of even those not directly affected was plummeting too.

Watching from the sidelines, I felt compelled to do something to help. I could absolutely empathise with the way that so many people were feeling. I felt similarly numerous times in my early adult life; indeed, the 'original' Gael who made a brief appearance that day, bursting into tears on hearing my daughter's news, is still inside me and will surface when I am highly stressed or shocked.

The crucial key to making the best of difficult times is, I believe, to look for the positive in change, however unwelcome it may seem. But I also know that this is much easier said than done, and that certain qualities and skills are needed to make it possible. Confidence, emotional resilience and motivation are required in order to be able to move on positively, but, by their very nature, difficult times will knock all three of these out of the best of us. I have written many self-help programmes designed to develop and strengthen them, but when a setback hits, most people have neither the time nor the energy to embark upon demanding plans for personal development. I knew I needed to offer a different kind of solution.

Mulling this over, I hit upon the idea for a book of tips that could give instant comfort and practical help. From years of helping people with an incredibly wide range of testing challenges, I know that the main qualities and skills needed to make the best of these are eminently transferable; and my work as a therapist and my own personal experiences have given me numerous tools and tricks to this end.

This book is the result – a new collection of tips and tools aimed specifically at addressing the problem of low morale during tough times. The stories and examples I have used as illustrations are based on a range of setbacks, such as: a heartbreaking separation or divorce; death of a loved one; redundancy or an earlier-than-anticipated retirement; the betrayal of trust by a friend; failure to pass an exam or secure a job that you wanted; lack of success in business or sport; a painful illness or other medical condition that restricts your lifestyle; being a survivor of a disaster or war.

Each of these challenges can knock back morale, largely because they almost always require a change that you had not bargained for or wanted. Some of us obviously cope better than others, but *all* human beings are instinctively frightened by the prospect of the unknown. Initially, many of us also feel powerless and ill-equipped to cope. But even if we are relatively adept at controlling this stress reaction, and can then deal constructively with the change, it is a process that takes time and when challenges come too close together (as they often do), anyone can feel overwhelmingly daunted.

Neuroscientists have warned that the human brain cannot evolve and adapt quickly enough to cope well with the pace of change that many of us are encountering today. Perhaps this is one of the main reasons why depression and anxiety disorders are on the increase.

So how does *101 Morale Boosters* counter all of that?

As the title suggests, there are 101 morale-boosting ideas for you to try, and you can approach them in several different ways. You can just dip in and out of the book whenever you need a quick pick-me-up – this works especially well if you already know what you should do, but just need a kick-start into doing it right now. Alternatively, you can target a particular area of need: you will see from the Contents that the tips are divided into ten sections, making it easy for you to access help for specific problems, such as a slump in confidence or motivation. Finally, if you are someone who suffers with chronic low morale, you can use the book as a self-help programme, working through it section by section. This can be particularly effective if you do it together with a friend or in a self-help group; you would then benefit from both giving and receiving the extra support and motivation.

Some of the tips are tried-and-tested favourite strategies which I have modified, others are new ideas. While the majority can be learnt quickly and applied immediately, some are more 'meaty', requiring a little more time to read and understand before they can be put into effective practice. Having said that, once you have read or worked on these longer tips, the next time you are in a challenging real-life situation, you will be able to apply what you have learnt very quickly.

None of us ever knows what life has in store for us or for our family and friends, but in order to emerge from setbacks stronger and more resilient, you need to keep your morale reserves continually topped up, using these tips even when your most testing time is over. This will give you a boost should you meet more difficult times in the future, as well as equipping you to help others through theirs.

I hope you find this collection of tips helpful and inspiring.

SECTION 1
Become Your Own 'Chief Comforter'

The emotional fallout you experience from whatever difficulties you have encountered is something that's often very difficult to deal with. One of the knock-on effects of ignoring emotional hurt is a loss of self-confidence and, consequently, morale. Buried feelings, especially deep ones, rarely just dissolve away. They have a tendency to leak or burst out and surprise you at inconvenient moments; or they may trigger physical issues, such as a loss of energy, headaches or, more seriously, problems with your heart or immune system. Unexpressed feelings are also bad for mental health and are frequently found at the root of problems such as depression and chronic anxiety.

This is why it is essential to deal with the emotional impact of whatever has happened to you as quickly as you can. If you have been made redundant, are facing divorce or have lost a parent, for example, you will probably need initially all the energy, confidence and inner calm you can muster to cope with the situation. Later, however, you may need them even more when it comes to making decisions about possible new paths in your life.

In my work as a therapist, I have identified five essential stages of the emotional-healing process. They are:

- exploring what has happened
- expressing triggered feelings in a safe way
- taking comfort from others (including yourself)
- compensating yourself
- taking a big-picture view of what's happened in order to gain perspective and learn from it.

Each stage is equally important and, when experienced in the right order, they should flow easily from one to the next. However, in your day-to-day rush, it's all too easy to skip steps or to get stuck in the process at some point. And even if you think you have already dealt with your feelings adequately, chances are that if your morale is low, you haven't spent enough time on these early stages of healing.

The tips in this section are designed to guide you through the emotional-healing process and, importantly, to help you find the time and space to put it into action.

> *The healing process takes personal courage, and a willingness to face things not always easy to face.*
> **Marianne Williamson, author and spiritual teacher**

Create a ten-minute hibernation haven

I think all I need is a few weeks of peace and I'll be fine . . . then I will be able to cope and know what I need to do.
Jane, recently deserted by her boyfriend and father of her two young children

Jane had been happily living with her boyfriend for nine years. Their children were aged two and a half and eighteen months when he proposed that they take the big leap and get married. In preparation, they decided to move into a new, larger flat. One Saturday afternoon, they went out looking at various properties. On their return, Jane's boyfriend told her that he had changed his mind and could not 'go through with it'. He gathered up his belongings, walked out and has not been back since.

Not surprisingly, when Jane came to see me months later, she was still unable to come to terms with this totally unanticipated and inexplicable change in her life. We couldn't even begin to plan her next step because she was overwhelmed by the stresses of her everyday life. She had become fixated on the idea of a holiday in isolation as her solution and, as is often the case, this was an impossible fantasy.

Do you, like Jane, often find yourself yearning for a means of escape from your here and now? This is a very natural and normal response to a shock or ongoing stress. Your mind is simply answering the physiological needs it is sensing. It is saying that your body and brain are exhausted. They are in serious need of a recharge.

It may be of some comfort to know that even if it were feasible, an escape holiday could well make matters worse. People who are 'lucky' enough to get away from it all on a sun-soaked beach or at a tranquil spa often find that on their return they feel even more sad, powerless or depressed than before.

A more positive alternative is to feed regularly the needs at the root of your yearning, and one way to do this is by creating an accessible haven in your home or office. This will allow you to take frequent mini-escapes in tranquillity which will cost you virtually nothing and take up very little of your precious problem-solving time. Regular ten-minute recharges in your haven will give you a much-needed energy boost in the short term, while in the long term, they will prevent a toxic build-up of the side effects of the stress hormones that render you more vulnerable to all manner of disease and infection.

No room for excuses!

You may well be saying or thinking: 'Nice idea . . . if only it were possible!' And this was Jane's first response, followed by a series of other 'excuses', before she finally agreed to have a go. So before we look at the practicalities of creating a haven, let's first deal with a few of the most common responses.

'There's no room or money for such a place'

Of course, ideally it would be wonderful to have a separate, sound-proofed room designed and equipped as a relaxation haven in every home and workplace. Such places do exist; I have seen and envied them. But they are a luxury that only a very privileged few can ever have, while the rest of us must create our haven within a room that serves many other purposes. This may initially require a little more imagination than a purpose-built haven, but the end result can be equally restorative.

'I'm far too busy and tired to take on anything else'

Saying this is a sure sign that you need an easy-to-use haven. You are at risk of both physical and mental ill health which would put even more pressure on your agenda and your body. Regular relaxation breaks in a very handy location are exactly what you need to keep your body and mind working well enough to support you through tough periods.

'I can't suddenly take over a space that belongs to others as well'

Of course you will need to negotiate with anyone else who has a right to use the space in question. But is that impossible? You would only need to use the haven area for periods of 10 minutes if it is well equipped and you become skilled at relaxation. Maybe others might join you when they witness the beneficial effect it has on you!

'Even if I had such a place I'd never use it . . . that's me'

You must believe that you can change. Certainly, your genetic inherited temperament and your past have shaped the personality traits you have today. But, by adopting new behavioural habits, you can both feel a different person and appear to be so to others. There is increasing evidence from recent neuroscience research which shows that if changes in behaviour are repeated frequently, new neural connections are created in the brain. This means that a 'new you' could become a physical reality. So if you want to be the kind of cool person who 'chills out' regularly, you can be.

How to create and use your haven

Let's assume that you do not have a spare room that could be used solely as your haven – a room that is used quite infrequently, perhaps for meetings or guests is an ideal alternative – with the help of a free-standing screen, one corner of a bedroom, sitting room or office can be left fully prepared for use as your haven. Or, if this too is impossible, with just a few simple props you can easily and quickly create a good-enough ambience in any room. And your props can be kept together in a small box, bag or chest that can travel with you wherever you go.

When choosing the equipment for your haven, focus on objects and furnishings that stimulate your senses rather than your intellect. Your senses have a fast-track route to the emotional centre in your brain.

Here is a list of some of the basics that you may want to include:

* **Comfortable seating:** the kind that allows you to lie with your back and neck supported and your feet up is ideal, but any chair will do with the help of a small back cushion (or rolled-up towel) and stool or other object on which to rest your legs.

* **Headphones:** preferably the noise-reduction kind that block out most external sounds.

* **Portable music player:** preloaded with music or sounds you find relaxing.

* **Low lighting:** a candle is ideal as the flicker of a flame is hypnotic. If you cannot dim the lights, have an eye mask to hand for some of the time. (Dim lighting stimulates the production of the hormone melatonin which helps to relax you in preparation for sleep.)

* **Relaxing and uplifting colours:** ensure that your favourite choice of both is in the furnishing or objects around you.

* **Scent:** choose ones which you associate with pleasure and relaxation, using room sprays, incense sticks, candles or burning oils or real scented flowers.

* **A few books containing pictures or photographs that have a soothing and pleasurable effect on you.** You could compile a special one with your own photos and postcards.

* **An alarm clock, timer or stopwatch** to ensure that you keep to your 10 minutes. If, for example, you should fall asleep and miss an important deadline, that would defeat the object of the exercise and you may never use your haven again.

Checklist for before using your haven

✔ Inform anyone who needs to know that you are not to be disturbed

✔ Prepare a nutritious snack and healthy drink

✔ Turn off your phones

✔ Go to the loo

✔ Darken and heat or cool the room to a comfortable body temperature; alternatively have a warm blanket or cooling, wet flannels available

✔ Light your perfumed candle or incense or spray your scent

Ten-minute programme for a haven break

1. **For 1 minute:** release tension from any taut muscles with some simple stretching exercises. Then, screw up your face, squeezing your eyes shut and letting out a big whoosh of breath when you release your muscles. Repeat a couple of times.

2. **For 4 minutes:** put on your headphones (with silence, music or sounds as you prefer), lie down or lounge and browse through one of your chosen books.

3. **For 4 minutes:** close your eyes or put on an eye mask; take three slow, deep breaths and allow yourself to sink into a physically and mentally relaxed state (see p. 121–4 for tips to help you do this). You should feel as though you are a floating zombie!

4. **For 1 minute:** do a few stretches, then briskly march on the spot to re-energise your system.

QUICK FIX: Cuddle yourself with comfy clothes

When I free my body from its clothes, from all their buttons, belts and laces, it seems to me that my soul takes a deeper, freer breath.
August Strindberg, playwright

If you are someone who feels more at ease in track-suits or other comfy clothes, why not apply this principle more liberally during tough times? Take a look at your wardrobe and view each garment in relation to its therapeutic qualities. Give each one a rating to reflect how good it is at helping you to feel relaxed or bringing a smile to your face through putting it on.

Most people find that their older outfits get the highest scores. So it should cost you precisely nothing to cuddle yourself more often in comfort clothing. Take a break from fashion and image slavery, and if you're worried about what others might think, remember the following wise words from fashion writer Lee Mildon: 'People seldom notice old clothes if you wear a big smile.'

Make a date with your duvet

There is nothing like staying at home for real comfort.

Jane Austen, novelist

Setting aside a day occasionally for cosseting yourself with pure self-indulgence will give both your health and self-esteem a boost.

Nowadays, it is a common belief that this is best achieved by booking a day at a luxury health spa. As wonderful as these can be, even if you can afford this kind of treat, when you are going through a particularly difficult time, it can be counterproductive. Spas are great venues, perhaps for celebrations and treats, but not the best places for emotional recovery, especially if you have financial worries. A quiet 'duvet day' in the comfort of your own home is usually much more beneficial.

The longer your duvet day is, the better will be its effects, but in practical terms, you may only be able to spare a few hours. If this is the case, it is even more important to prepare for it carefully so you can make the very most of it. Here are some suggestions to include on your to-do list:

* Make arrangements for your home to be emptied of everyone. This is a day just for you, regardless of how close you are to others. The pleasure and healing you get from togetherness is wonderful, but different. A day of self-indulgence in solitude offers other possibilities. It gives you the freedom to be exactly who you are; think about whatever comes into your mind, however stupid, illogical or disgraceful those thoughts may seem, and,

of course, to do whatever you want to do, even if that is nothing.

* If you have to ask for help to make your solitude possible, remember that you can return favours later; giving back to someone else in their hour of need is so pleasurable that you will receive a bonus mood-booster.

* Fill your fridge with nutritious bite-sized treats and healthy drinks. In particular, make sure you have all you need for a luxurious breakfast in bed, as this will put you in the correct self-indulgent mood. If you prefer to cook and prepare these yourself, do as much of the work as you can the day before. Duvet days are lazy days.

* Inform anyone who is likely to call or visit that you are having an 'away day'. If a little white lie is necessary, simply say in a brisk tone that you have some personal matters to attend to. This will protect your privacy, as it tends to block further questions.

* Prepare your own entertainment, so that you are not relying on daytime TV to amuse you. I have heard so many people express regrets about watching 'rubbish' all day that I think it is worth having a special selection of DVDs or videos to hand. Old favourites with a high feel-good factor or ones that make you laugh are always a safe option.

* Select a range of music that is relaxing and also some to use at the end of your 'day' to uplift your mood and energise you. Remember, this is also an opportunity for you to enjoy to your heart's content all that music that irritates or bores others in your life.

QUICK FIX: Take a five-minute dose of soothing silence

> *There is no need to go to India or anywhere else to find peace. You will find that deep place of silence right in your room, your garden or even your bathtub.*
> **Elizabeth Kubler-Ross, psychiatrist, author and innovative leader in the hospice movement**

Research carried out by Theodore Wachs, a professor of psychological sciences at Purdue University in the US, has revealed that children who come from highly noisy or chaotic homes experience less cognitive growth, delayed language skills, have trouble mastering their environments and have increased anxiety. Other research has proved that constant noise affects both physical and mental health to such a degree that many governments now have legislation and special departments in place to control it.

In today's world, there are very few accessible places where silence can be readily found. But you can create it for yourself, even if it takes earplugs plus noise-reducing headphones and triple-glazing to do so.

* If you love reading, buy or borrow a book that you know will absorb your attention and offer some distraction from your problems. This is not the time for self-help books or any offering possible solutions. Put these aside until your morale is stronger and you are feeling more optimistic and motivated. Your concentration is

probably not at its best so all those collections of inspirational quotes, quirky facts, cartoons or jokes that usually only see the light of day at Christmas time are ideal.

* Consider buying a cheap pay-as-you-go phone and give the number to only a few people whom you would want to contact you in an emergency. This will leave you free to turn off all other communication with the outside world, not just on your duvet day, but at many other times as well.

 ## Establish reassuring rituals

Do you remember how soothing rituals felt when you were a child? As a parent, I admit that I sometimes felt excruciatingly bored reading the same bedtime story, singing the same tunes and hearing the same jokes over and over again. But that was what my children demanded, and I soon learnt the advantages of giving in.

Rituals undoubtedly have a calming power. And it's not just harassed parents who find them useful. Religious leaders, for example, often use familiar ceremonies and songs to get their 'audiences' into a calm (and therefore more receptive) frame of mind before giving important sermons or addresses.

Recently, while giving a talk at a business networking event, I mentioned something about the calming nature of rituals, and one of the executives there, Peter – a senior board member of a large company – shared his story with me:

Over a period of months Peter had had to be involved in high-level extremely confidential discussions with colleagues, lawyers and accountants about the company's dwindling profits and cutback plans. Unlike many of his fellow board members, Peter had been with the company for much of his career. He knew and admired the founder – a benevolent and caring employer who had often told the then novice manager Peter that, 'Nurturing and retaining staff is the key to long-term success.'

Outside the boardroom during these months Peter had to act as though nothing had or would change. Internally, he was going through emotional hell. He knew that just before Christmas the announcement of major job losses would be made and redundancy would follow very rapidly for many hundreds of excellent workers whom he knew had major financial and family responsibilities. Peter was on an emotional rollercoaster of sadness, anger, guilt and shame. He could not even share these feelings with his wife, as many of those in the firing line were also personal family friends.

One morning, as Peter was showering, for no apparent reason he remembered an old ritual he used to start the day with before his work life had become so pressurised. He had taken a daily walk which he felt helped him to separate the two worlds of family and work. He would sidestep off the quickest route and go through a park and over the river bridge. While doing this, he listened to music on a pocket radio. Just before he reached the office he would treat himself to a cappuccino and fresh croissant in a small Italian café. While there, he enjoyed striking up conversations with many of the café's regular customers.

With this memory in mind, Peter bought himself a mini MP3 player and restarted his 'ritual'. He claims that it helped him to 'keep his head' through a very tough patch and that it continues to do so!

Researchers at Harvard medical school have found that rituals can even be used as a placebo to relieve pain. Maybe this is why my gentle exercise ritual each morning is so effective. If it is not preceded by my usual cup of jasmine tea in bed and then done to the accompaniment of a certain radio programme, my aching muscles never appear to get the same relief!

Try establishing one or two new rituals to help you cope. Choose ones that you enjoy and help you to feel relaxed as well. Here are some simple examples that others say are helpful:

Examples of easy-to-do rituals

* Take 10 minutes at a certain time mid-morning to sit with a coffee and read the paper.

* Go out for a short walk alone after lunch each day.

* Listen to a favourite radio programme while having a bath.

* Get together with the family for a meal or snack at more or less the same time each day (one of my favourites).

* Take a break on return from work, shopping or taking the children to school to listen to or play music.

* Go to the cinema or watch a DVD every Friday night.

* Meet up with friends in the same pub once a month.

You may already have your own similar kind of calming ritual activity. If so, stick fast with what you already know helps you, but do try to ensure that it doesn't get sidelined as can so often happen in the hurly-burly of difficult times.

Finally, remember that there is a difference between a routine that you want to do and one that has just become a purposeless boring habit. So the same series of actions can be a comforting ritual for one person and a morale knock-back for someone else – in the words of Dwight Currie, author of the bestselling book *How We Behave at the Feast: Reflections on Living in an Age of Plenty*: 'One man's rut is another man's ritual.'

Add bursts of beauty to the backdrop of your life

When you have only two pennies left in the world, buy a loaf of bread with one and a lily with the other.
Chinese proverb

Recently, I met a friend for coffee whom I hadn't seen for a couple of months. The moment I saw her, I commented on how *great* she looked. I could see she was a bit taken aback by the intensity of my tone (she did, in fact, look years younger than when I had last seen her), and she was curious to know what it was about her that had made such an impression on me – whether it was what she was wearing, for example. But it had nothing to do with her clothes; she had on an outfit I had seen her wear many times before. Confronted with specifying exactly what had prompted my remark, I said perhaps it was the sparkle in her eyes, her beaming smile, glowing skin and her relaxed and easy posture, all of which formed quite a different picture from the one I had seen last time we'd met.

My friend explained that over the previous months her work had become extremely pressurised. In addition, as she was nearing retirement, she had been having major anxieties about the sudden and unexpected erosion of her pension caused by the economic downturn.

As we talked, I expected to hear some good news about a change in her circumstances. But no, her stresses were greater than ever. The conversation then moved on to sharing news about our recent activities, and it became clear what had caused such a noticeable lift in my friend's demeanour and appearance. She mentioned that she had recently spent a weekend in Paris which had set her thinking. While she was there, she had done nothing particularly special or unusual. She had just walked around, looking at buildings and visiting a few galleries. But on her return, she found that she felt very different. She said she was convinced that it was simply the beauty of Paris that had lifted her mood and relaxed her body and mind. It made her realise how little time she had been spending around beauty and that she had forgotten what a powerful tonic it is for her. Since her return, she'd been setting aside time to enjoy regular 'doses' of beauty, for example, taking a walk on a cliff top with stunning views, seeing a beautifully filmed movie and going on a guided tour of a well-known gallery that opened her eyes to some striking art she had never noticed before.

No wonder my friend looked so much better! Beauty is a natural stimulator of the happiness hormones. The chemical response that it sets off within us infuses us with a sense of wellbeing. It helps muscles to relax, dulls physical pain and causes mental worries to float automatically to the back of your mind.

And, of course, as my friend found on her return home, you don't need to rush off to Paris to get this kind of fix. Beauty is always available for you to enjoy in your day-to-day life. You may simply need to make a conscious effort to notice it and allow yourself a little time to appreciate it. When you are stressed, your mind is even less likely to pick up automatically on these everyday opportunities to benefit from the restorative pleasure of beauty.

One way to counter this effect of stress is to reignite your 'beauty sensors' by regularly adding new and unusual stimulants into the backdrop of your life. Of course, how you choose to do this will vary from individual to individual. I might use visually stimulating pictures, for example, while my husband is more likely to listen to an uplifting piece of music. One friend of mine would choose to feel a delicately textured fabric, while another would select a fresh fragrance from a garden.

Cheap and easy ways to add bursts of beauty to everyday life

* Buy yourself flowers or a plant each month.

* Put a new beautiful photo on to your screen saver each week.

* Borrow an art book from the library once a week.

* Collect postcards from museums and galleries or card shops and mount regular new art shows on your kitchen cupboards or around your desk.

* Collect different leaves and draw or press inside a book and then paste on to a card and send to friends.

* Collect recommended recipes and cook a new one at least once a month.

* Gather together small pieces of fabric with different textures from remnant boxes or old clothes and make into a collage or scarf that you can feel and enjoy.

* Make a collection of stones or shells and wash and polish each in turn.

* Collect a few worms and earth in a jar and observe them for a day or so.

* Visit a butterfly museum (there is a wonderful one in Portsmouth in the UK).

* Take a walk in a rose garden and drink in each of the individual scents, one by one.

* Take a few minutes each day to notice the evolving colours and shapes of the sky.

QUICK FIX: Feel your feelings

Use this tip regularly to release pent-up emotion in a gentle and safe way.

1. Find a quiet space, either alone or with someone you can be yourself with.

2. Close your eyes and take a few deep, slow breaths.

3. Focus your mind on your emotional state for about 1 minute; notice the sensations in your body.

4. Let yourself express these for 20 seconds or so – allow tears of sadness and disappointment to well up; let out a growl of anger; shudder out your fear or anxiety.

5. Take another three deep, slow breaths while mentally focusing on the passage of your breath.

6. Have a comfort experience: if you are with someone, share your feelings and take any comfort offered (but don't get into further discussion which could unbalance you emotionally); if you are alone, give yourself a small, comforting treat.

Note: if this exercise reveals deep or conflicting feelings, make a note to deal with them later, so you can keep your feelings under control while you resolve your current problem, then re-examine them once you are feeling more confident; *The Emotional Healing Strategy* (see Resources, p. 265) can help with this.

You can get many more ideas by reading or questioning people around you on this subject. Poets and young children can be great sources of inspiration as they see wondrous beauty in things that so often become 'ordinary' and go unnoticed.

After finding out what others appreciate in an object or experience, make a conscious effort to be open to sensing the beauty that is able to give them so much pleasure. It doesn't always work, but when it does I find it very exciting. There was a time I never could have imagined finding myself uplifted by the beauty of a gliding snail in the garden or the sky in a wild Yorkshire storm, for example.

> *The moment one gives close attention to anything,*
> *even a blade of grass, it becomes*
> *a mysterious, awesome, indescribably*
> *magnificent world in itself.*
> **Henry Miller, playwright**

 ## Check 'cold comfort' habits

Comforting treats must become a staple psychological food during difficult times. When you need emotional healing after a disappointment, injustice or setback, you should grant yourself an even larger helping. But be very careful not to choose the kind which I call 'sting-in-the tail' treats – those which may feel instantly good, but which have a knock-on negative side effect. This is a very common habit among people whose mood is already depressed.

Rebecca was finding it very hard to move on after her relationship with her boyfriend had ended. One of the main reasons was that she could not face being hurt again. She had seen my book *The Emotional Healing Strategy*, and came to me for a few 'booster' sessions. As we explored her problem, it became obvious that the comfort stage was where she was going wrong. The only examples she could give me of ways with which she could comfort herself after a rejection were what she termed as 'naughty foods', such as chocolates and coconut ice cream. As she had struggled for many years with weight issues, these were sting-in-the-tail treats that could never be truly comforting to her.

A sting-in-the-tail treat could have a detrimental effect on your health, affect your concentration at work the next day, diminish your struggling bank balance or irritate your partner. In the long term, therefore, they are likely to be counterproductive because they produce extra trouble and stress. Many are also guaranteed to make you feel guilty, just as Rebecca's did, and so will eat away at your self-esteem.

> *There's no better way to energise your body, mind and spirit than by taking care of yourself.*
> **Stephanie Tourles, holistic beautician and author**

Learn to identify the sting in the tail

Here are some common examples to start you off on making your own 'bad treats' warning list. It is a good idea to let anyone who might want to help you have some comfort look at your list too. You could also ask them to help you compile a list of good-for-you alternatives.

Comfort treat	Possible stings in the tail
Drowning your sorrows	A hangover; saying or doing things you'll regret; liver damage
Sugar fixes	Weight gain; bad teeth; increased diabetes risk
Retail therapy	Unnecessary impulse buys; credit card debt
Cheap weekend break	Exhausting travel and sight-seeing; bad food; dingy hotel
Expensive bouquets	Flowers die quickly; cost five times the price of a simple bunch of fresher flowers
Restaurant meal	Time-consuming; less nutritious; annoying music; overeating (usually); exorbitant wine

Plan to compensate yourself

*If we will be quiet and ready enough, we shall
find compensation in every disappointment.*
Henry David Thoreau, philosopher

Sean, a pilot in the Spanish air force, had a heart bypass
at the age of forty-five. He was then placed on indefinite
sick leave, although on recovery from the operation he
felt as fit and able as he had been at thirty-nine. Many
people might have welcomed this enforced retirement,
but for Sean it was a blow which threw him and his

relationship with his family whom he dearly loved into turmoil. He missed his work. The pressure had been high, but it had always been exciting. He also missed the camaraderie of his colleagues, his status and responsibility and the travel.

For Sean's family, the adjustment was hard too. They were not used to having him at home. He had three teenage children, all at different stages of testing the boundaries of parental patience. The setting of house rules and discipline had previously been the province of Sean's wife, together with her mother, who had effectively become the co-parent as she looked after the children much of the time. Both women now found Sean's intervention in their 'zone of control' hard. The children (as is normal with teenagers) were quick to take advantage of the mismatch in the differing rules and degrees of willingness to part with money.

Sean could see no way out of this stressful situation. The family, including him, were too set in their ways to change much. He knew he needed more time out of the house, but another job was impossible as he would lose his sick pay. He had not built up a social life or any absorbing hobbies in his home town. His buddies were scattered across Spain and much of the world. The friends of the family had inevitably been chosen by his wife and Sean felt on the outside of this closely bonded group.

After a serious heart-to-heart talk, Sean and his wife agreed that he should go and stay with one of his close colleagues who happened to be on leave for a few weeks. This colleague was staying in a recently bought seaside apartment which happened to adjoin a golf course. Neither Sean nor his colleague had ever been interested in golf, but a neighbour invited them to join him at his club for a round. This was the start of a passion that probably saved Sean's marriage. It very quickly became apparent that Sean had innate golfing talents. With his friend's encouragement, he decided to treat himself to twenty lessons with a professional and membership of his local club on his return home. They agreed he deserved to spend this money on himself as compensation for having lost the working and social life that he had loved.

QUICK FIX: Give yourself a 'gratitude gift'

This tip may well sound like over-the-top self-indulgence but trust me, it works! I first suggested it to someone who was feeling very low about Christmas, as she had just got divorced. It worked so well as a boost that I have used the idea many times since and for different reasons.

I suggest that you use this tip now to say 'thank you' to yourself for being self-comforting. After all, if someone else has been particularly kind to you, you would think it perfectly natural to give them a small gift to express your gratitude. So why not buy yourself a small symbolic gift as a 'Thank you to me for having been more self-nurturing'. You'll find it is a great mood-lifter and motivator. And, if you still feel it is too much of an odd thing to do, just try doing a search on the Internet for 'Gifts for you'. You'll see that there is quite a large market for people who want to do it.

Compensating yourself for the emotional hurt you have suffered is an essential step in the psychological healing process. Very often, in difficult times you can be so involved in sorting out practical issues that your emotional-health needs are neglected. The only compensation that is likely to be given priority is the financial kind, if that is possible. But the type of compensation that I believe gives a truly satisfying emotional and morale lift is that which Sean gave himself. The golf idea worked because it fitted with the hurt that he had felt by being retired so early. It boosted his self-esteem, as it was using his best talents, gave him a friendship circle with men that he missed and gave him and his family the opportunity to get back to playing the roles that had worked so well for them all for many years.

What kind of compensation might work for you?

The key to choosing well is to think of the deficit or deficits that your setback has left you with. These can be psychological, material, financial, social, personal growth or health issues. Very often, it is a mixed bag of a few of these. But for the purposes of compensation, selecting one key area may work well enough for emotional healing. Here are some examples to start you thinking:

Deficit	Loss of trust in a friendship
Compensation	Join a club to meet new friends
Deficit	Loss of optimistic outlook
Compensation	Books of encouraging quotes; DVDs of films about inspirational people

Deficit	Physical ability
Compensation	Interest or hobby that develops mental strengths
Deficit	Self-esteem
Compensation	Overdose on the mini-boosts listed on pages 40–2
Deficit	Loss of garden due to repossession of house
Compensation	A flat adjacent to a beautiful park that is maintained by someone else

SECTION 2
Boost Your Self-confidence

No one is immune to having their self-confidence knocked a little at some time during a difficult period. Even when a setback is not due to any personal failure, the prospect of change can create an internal wobble of self-doubt.

For those of you who may already have a good deal of confidence, these tips can therefore just serve as a reminder – as in the heat of a challenge, the habit of continually nurturing confidence can slip. For others, however, they might prove to be a more fundamental eye-opener to confidence-building. Commonly, most people who lack this much-envied quality find it hard to believe that they can make such a major change to their personality. And this *mistaken* belief makes it even harder for them to have faith that they can get through difficult times.

Most of the tips in this section focus on feeding self-esteem. This lies at the heart of self-confidence and you need it in abundance when you are faced with big challenges. You cannot overdose on these tips; they will not make you arrogant or selfish. Neither will they infuse you with a false conviction that you can achieve absolutely anything you set your mind to. But they will give you a more positive belief in yourself than I imagine you may already have, and keep this vital certainty burning brightly, so that you have hope and confidence when you most need them.

This section also includes tips designed to extend your self-knowledge and keep your focus moving positively forward, preventing you from being too hard on yourself over any past failures or current weaknesses.

Play to your strengths

When I dare to be powerful, to use my strength in the service of my vision, then it becomes less and less important whether I am afraid.
Audre Lorde, poet

We all have our own unique package of personal strengths, and one of the big secrets of confident people is that they know precisely what is in their package and how to use each strength to advantage in any given situation. In contrast, people who lack confidence are super-aware of their weaknesses and spend most of their energy on either attempting to improve these or hide them.

Your self-confidence has probably been rocked by whatever problem you have right now. You need to give it some boosts. This exercise will help by reminding you how you can use your strengths to help you in this situation. If you struggle to come up with enough examples of your strengths, seek help from a good friend immediately. It is crucial to confidence to be able to keep your best inner resources at the forefront of your mind.

List three to six of your personal strengths in each of the following categories and beside each one note down how they could help get you through this difficult period. The example will give you an idea of how to do this exercise, but remember that your strengths may be very different (although no less useful).

My innate talents and aptitudes

Musical

Helps to relax or energise me; strengthen social contacts by giving free pleasure to others.

An accurate eye

Tennis – keeps me fit and releases tension; can make new contacts at club.

Creativity

Can draw my own Christmas card to save money; revamp the sitting room cheaply to boost my mood; use painting to relax me; drama to practise interview skills.

My core character strengths

Persistence

Can keep going even when I become bored or tired, so I could do a boring, fill-in job while waiting; I can fight through bureaucracy to check my full entitlement to help.

Sense of humour

Can cheer up others; keep my perspective; divert my attention from worry.

Optimism

Can spot opportunities; keep self and others motivated.

My special skills

IT	Opens research possibilities; can network more widely; work from home or anywhere in the world; on-line courses.
Selling	Can promote myself; apply for wider range of jobs; get best price for flat if we need to sell.
Listening	Can make new friends; elicit ideas from others; collaborate with others in the same boat.
Numeracy	Helps with redoing the budget; calculating real value of bargain; offering to be treasurer of resident's association and gain more power over decision-making.
Cooking	Diversion from problems; make interesting meals from cheap ingredients; sell homemade cakes/jams and sauces or use for presents; entertain possible good contacts.
Project management	View this problem as a project with a start and finish point; keep organised and focused; review progress.

QUICK FIX: Celebrate the uncelebrated

Few people celebrate their achievements adequately. Normally, only certain successes are routinely deemed worthy of celebration, such as passed exams, new jobs or winning competitions. However, in the field of personal development, these may not be the achievements that people consider to be their greatest. Here are some examples of what people have told me they regard as achievements – none of them was celebrated at the time, but they certainly deserve to be:

* Being a good parent
* Having a good relationship with your partner
* Keeping the peace with the in-laws
* Becoming fluent in a language
* Mastering the computer
* Going solo on holiday
* Getting over a divorce or separation
* Overcoming a fear of flying
* Growing roses in unfriendly soil
* Making a beautiful home
* Learning how to keep cool with the boss
* Becoming well organised instead of living in chaos
* Becoming a good manager or leader

This should prompt a belated celebration for some of your own achievements!

Feed a psychological need

This is a great tip if you are in a panic about something. Perhaps your working life is threatened or your income could be drastically reduced for some other reason? Very often there is a period of time when you are powerless to do anything about a worrying situation other than wait, whether for news of a job or another change of financial wind.

But what you can do instead is to focus on feeding your psychological needs. This will divert your attention from your concerns about your material wealth, while strengthening your psychological health.

Here are some examples of psychological needs and how they can be 'fed', simply by using the tips in this book. But remember, there are many other psychological needs and many other low-cost and quick ways to fulfil them.

Psychological need	Fulfilling tip
Achievement	Revive a hidden talent (p. 39)
Companionship	Deepen your key relationships (p. 203)
Adventure	Experiment with eccentricity (p. 46)
Status	Invest more time in your community (p. 212)
Self-esteem	Drip-feed your self-esteem with mini-boosts (pp. 40–2)

Reassurance	Use imaginary mentors to psych you up (p. 241)
Solitude	Create a ten-minute hibernation haven (p. 5)
Self-expression	Stimulate your spontaneity and creativity with an artistic challenge (p. 130)
Self-determination	Strengthen your self-reliance (p. 52)

 # Revive a hidden talent

Adversity has the effect of eliciting talents which, in prosperous circumstances would have lain dormant.
Horace, Roman poet and philosopher

Joyce, my Spanish teacher and friend, was diagnosed with Parkinson's disease in her early forties. For the first couple of months she was in a state of shock and very worried about her future. But then her positive fighting nature kicked back in again. She found out as much as she could about the disease and learnt that she could ameliorate her symptoms considerably if she exercised.

In her younger years she'd had a talent for crafts and decided to start that hobby again. She now makes the most beautiful cards and framed pictures using intricate paper 'sculptures' and calligraphy, and gives them as presents to friends. This work has improved the mobility of her fingers and hands considerably. I have one of her pictures in my office by my computer, and it is a constant source of inspiration.

Do you have a talent for art or a hobby or sport that has fallen by the wayside – something that you could revive right now? If you can't think of one, perhaps you have another kind of talent that is underused, such as organising parties or speaking a language?

 # Drip-feed your self-esteem with mini-boosts

Most people don't realise that self-esteem is knocked back more by everyday events than by the big setbacks in life. For example, we can get used to being herded like cattle into trains, being ignored by shop attendants chatting to their friends or being left hanging on the end of the phone for 15 minutes. This kind of disrespect is so common and so impersonal that – sadly – it is rarely worth the hassle to 'fight back'. But it takes its toll, nevertheless. You can negate the emotional damage it causes, however, by counteracting it with equally regular mini-boosts which will instantly lift your self-esteem. Here are some examples:

Share good news however small

Ring a good friend and tell them about a mini-achievement, such as clearing your pending file, a spring clean, revamping your CV or resisting a temptation.

Give yourself a treat each day

This could be a favourite food or drink, a walk in a garden, a ten-minute break to read or listen to music. Remember to vary the experiences though, otherwise they will begin to feel too routine.

Log your achievements

Writing down on paper or on the computer what you have achieved each day or week will fix these achievements more firmly in your brain; include both personal and work-related ones.

Spruce up your appearance even when you are solo

Make those glances in the mirror or reflections in shop windows as uplifting as they can be.

Keep photos of people who love you visible

Swap the positions of these from time to time so you notice them more.

Give compliments more freely

Find reasons to compliment others, but make sure they are genuine and not too general. The smile of the receiver will boost you too.

Make a saving

Say 'No' to buying something you don't really need or wasting time, money and energy on doing something you don't need to do.

Share your empathy non-verbally

Just giving a sympathetic smile or raised eyebrows and a shake of the head to someone who looks sad or who has been treated disrespectfully can lift both your spirits and theirs. A few words may help too, but often they are not necessary and may not be appropriate.

Be kinder to your weaknesses

Our strength grows out of our weaknesses.
Ralph Waldo Emerson, American poet and essayist

When you are feeling low and anxious, your weaknesses tend to leap to the forefront of your mind, and, as a result, you may frequently find yourself blaming them for the mess and stress in your life.

> Gerry, a senior manager, had recently been made redundant. At one level in his mind, Gerry knew that the decision to cut his post had been purely made on cost-cutting grounds. But you'd find this difficult to believe if you took his self-accusatory ramblings at face value:
>
> 'I don't know what it is about me . . . I was the oldest person in the office and I know that my age was against me fitting in. But this is not the first time my job has been axed. I thought I was doing reasonably OK this time, but perhaps I'm not cut out for top management. I'm too soft for my own good . . . Even my wife says that about the way I am with the kids. But I've never been any good at playing tough. I should have seen this coming and been looking elsewhere for opportunities . . . but then I have

never been one for networking and office politics. You see I'm a bit of a workaholic and never have time for the things you're supposed to do for career development . . . and I'm not that good at those work–social events, anyway. I'm one of those that gets stuck in the corner with the office bore.

I have heard so many different variations on this kind of derogatory self-talk – from people whose hearts have been broken by partners who consistently cheated and lied, from parents whose dyslexic children have failed exams or from teenagers whose parents have died in an accident or of a terminal illness, for example.

There is of course a reason why this self-defeating habit sets in during difficult times. It is caused by that inevitable dip in self-esteem that accompanies problems that make us feel powerless. If you find yourself thinking or talking like Gerry, you might find that logical reasoning alone does nothing to budge this habit. So the next time someone responds to your self-blaming by kindly reminding you of the real reason for your difficulties and you still don't feel convinced, try following this mini 'CARE' strategy that got Gerry back on a positive track. It will help you to do something constructive about your weaknesses and make a more rational assessment of the part they may have played in your current situation.

CARE strategy for weaknesses

Step 1: *Care*

Indulge yourself with some quality, sensual self-nurturing. This will distract your attention away from your weaknesses, reboot your self-esteem and reset your mind into a positive mode. Refer to Section 1 in this book if you're not sure how to do this!

Step 2: Action

Now make some serious resolutions. This will help you take constructive action to correct the weaknesses which can be changed or become more accepting of those you must learn to live with.

Draw two columns on a piece of paper. In the first, write out a list of your weaknesses and in the second note down the action you intend to take in relation to them. There will be some that you wish to work on because they are hindering your progress or damaging your self-esteem, but there will be others that you may wish to merely accept and find a more comfortable way of living with or avoiding situations where they might hold you back.

Here's Gerry's list:

Weakness	*Action*
Age	Accept and focus on its benefits, e.g. wisdom
Being too soft with people	Assertiveness training
Shy – not good in big groups	Accept and do one-to-one and small-group networking; avoid big social events
Workaholic	Make firm rules about working hours and ask colleagues to help you abide by them

Step 3: *Reappraise*

Having engaged your rational mind and uplifted your mood you will be better placed to assess the true bearing your weaknesses have on your current situation. Draw a pie chart indicating the proportion of responsibility for your current problems that should be allocated to your weaknesses.

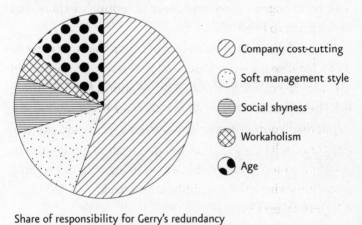

Company cost-cutting

Soft management style

Social shyness

Workaholism

Age

Share of responsibility for Gerry's redundancy

Step 4: *Extol*

Finally, you need to reboot your self-esteem and rebalance your view of yourself. A quick way to achieve this is to do a little private boasting about your virtues. Read aloud the list of strengths you compiled on pp. 35–6. Then finish by stating (again out loud) some of the positive action you have already taken to pull yourself through this tough patch in your life. Overleaf are Gerry's lists of strengths and achievements as an example.

Gerry's strengths

✔ I face up to problems and snap into action fast.

✔ I am kind and helpful.

✔ I am prepared to learn and adapt to changing circumstances.

✔ I have a great sense of humour and can amuse others.

✔ I have survived many other setbacks and learnt from them.

Gerry's achievements since being made redundant

✔ I have allowed myself time to recover emotionally and physically from the shock and stress.

✔ I have asked for help in spite of my embarrassment about asking for it.

✔ I have started to do an appraisal of my finances (or career opportunities or social situation etc.).

✔ I am dealing more constructively with my weaknesses.

Experiment with eccentricity

Nobody realises that some people expend tremendous energy merely trying to be normal.
Albert Camus, writer and philosopher

It can be very enlightening and energising to edge ourselves out of our character ruts from time to time. When life is going fine, we may do this purely for fun at Halloween or on a trip to Disneyland. But during tough times a push outside our comfortable character zone can be incredibly helpful.

Problem situations often require you to act and think in ways that are unusual for you. This exercise is one that I have used for many years with clients and it has proved to be a great confidence-builder for them, as well as giving insight into hidden or forgotten aspects of their personalities. Remember that it should be fun and that it won't do your self-esteem any good if you do something which offends others.

Here are a few examples to start you thinking.

Go 'shopping' without money

Take a small amount of emergency cash with you, but no credit cards. You can then feel free to experiment with trying on clothes to your heart's content. I once tried this out and learnt from it. I was trying on a hat that I thought looked hilariously stupid on me. Yet I was told in all seriousness by a couple of shoppers that it suited me. This made me realise that I had become a bit too 'reserved' in the way I dress. In my younger days, I had quite a reputation for wearing eye-catching clothes and had had fun wearing them.

Buy and wear an unusual accessory

Second-hand shops and stalls are a great place to find these cheaply. Buy them and wear them with panache at some event. One senior executive client wore a tie which had Rudolph the Reindeer's nose flashing red to the office party. This was very out of character for him and a positive surprise for those who thought they knew him well.

Order an unusual breakfast in a café

Another client of mine ordered an ice-cream dessert for breakfast in the middle of winter. As a result, he received some good-humoured teasing from the waiter and fellow eaters. This was great for him because he had slipped into becoming overly serious as a result of his difficulties. Lightening up didn't improve his bank balance, but it didn't diminish it either, and his wife appreciated the return of his sense of humour.

Activate the team potential within you

With different people and in different situations most of us can behave and feel quite differently. Indeed the differences can be so great that sometimes it feels as though we are a variety of different people rather than just one person. Take these people, for example:

> 'You should see me at work – I'm "Mr Fix-it" there. I'm a different person. I manage a team and a tight budget. At home, my wife sorts out and plans everything. She says I'm better playing with the children because I can't organise anything without forgetting something important or annoying someone.'

> 'My friends say I'm a great listener and they all come to me with their problems. But with my boyfriend, I'm

different. Sounds dreadful but I have no patience when he's down and my sister says I'm the same with her.'

'Looking at the 360-degree feedback from my colleagues, you'd think I had no sense of humour. They seem to think I'm too serious. Yet my friends call me the joker in their pack.'

'You should have seen me haggling in the market in Tangiers last year. I was the ace negotiator then. So why do I always end up giving in to the kids?'

There are many good reasons for being different people in different situations. For example, some aspects of personality are more appropriate to what you are trying to achieve, others are simply a better 'fit' with what another person needs from you, and sometimes it is just more relaxing to switch into a different mode. Compartmentalising yourself in this way may be fine while things are going well. In difficult times, however, you need to work on full capacity. You cannot afford to sideline any of your strengths and skills and should aim for them all to be functioning in co-ordination with each other.

An interesting and fun way of doing this is to think of your different 'selves' as a team. As any good team leader knows, the art of success is to create a group of people with different aptitudes and talents. This is because most problems need a variety of approaches and skills and also because a diverse team is usually better at coming up with new ideas. But a good manager will ensure that the team has plenty of everyday practice working constructively together before sending them into a 'fire-fighting' situation.

The exercise below is designed to help you to apply this team-training approach to the different parts of yourself. Repeat it a number of times with different examples; the principles will then stick fast in your brain so that your 'team' is ready for action whenever it meets a challenge.

Getting your inner team into action

Make a list of the different 'people' you have within your personality. Next, choose an everyday real-life or hypothetical problem for them to sort out together. Assign a task to each 'person' according to their special aptitudes or talents as in the example below.

Sample problem

My computer has crashed again. Is it worth upgrading to a new one, even though I'm strapped for cash right now? My IT knowledge is virtually nil – I dread the hassle of making this decision.

Plan

Your caring listener

Allow yourself to let off steam by kicking around some cushions and having a good 'It's-not-fair' moan. Then plan a small comforting treat for now and an enticing reward for when you have made your decision!

Your helpful humourist

Get the problem into proportion by doodling a cartoon about yourself and your panic over it.

Your clever intellectual
Research the Internet for various options of new computers; gather feedback and assess its value.

Your friendly social networker
Search among your contacts for IT specialists who may have advice or other contacts; go to a computer shop and start up conversation with staff or customers who look at home; talk a 'knowledgeable someone' into acting as your negotiator if you need one.

Your creative artist
Compose a colourful email that will have impact and instant appeal to friends and colleagues for help and advice.

Your sensible budgeter
Calculate comparative costs of different models and repair costs of current model and different interest on loans. Look at making cuts in other expenses.

Your efficient organiser/leader/manager
Do a timed action plan for your inner team. (They can't all act at once!) Set a deadline for decision time. When all tasks are done if you still can't make the decision yourself, delegate the task to someone you trust who can and give your reward to them instead.

Strengthen your self-reliance

When a crisis hits are you more likely to:

A) immediately turn to someone else, saying 'Help . . . what should I do?'

or

B) go quiet and think to yourself, 'Hell, how do I get through this?'

I know for sure that when I am faced with a big problem and thrown into my autopilot mode I am a B responder. This programmed character trait is another legacy of my childhood. I had to frequently fend for myself at a very early age, so developed a strong self-reliant streak which has undoubtedly helped me to bounce back from the many serious setbacks I have experienced. Interestingly, research findings show that the most likely people to survive disasters are those who do not expect to be rescued. They are the people who, in the heat of the crisis, automatically respond (as I am sure I would) with the thought: 'What can I do to save myself in this situation?'

If you are more of an A responder, however, don't worry too much. You have one big advantage in that you find it easy and natural to ask for and use help. In the early days of a big crisis, such as immediately after bereavement, this is especially valuable. It gives you time to recoup your physical and emotional strength, while others get on with sorting out at least some of your preliminary practical problems.

Of course, unfortunately, help and support have a habit of gradually dwindling away if a problem situation drags on for any length of time. This is especially true in today's individualistic, competitive and busy world. Even the kindest of 'helpers' have to (or feel they have to) keep their compassion in check. Almost every casualty of bereavement, chronic sickness, redundancy or divorce that I have ever met talks about this phenomenon. And it is at this point in a problematic situation that you most need to be able to draw on self-reliance. Those who will not readily accept this fact of modern life and cannot switch themselves into B mode are in danger of sliding into a powerless state. Feeling abandoned and rejected, they can become depressed, cynical and bitter. And, of course, these kinds of mental states do nothing at all to help them thrive or even survive through difficulties.

How to switch yourself into self-reliance mode

Think twice before asking for help or advice

This sounds obvious, but you may be stuck in a habit and not realise how often you do this – and how unnecessarily. To remind yourself, put some sticky notes around your home, near your phones or computer or wherever else you think it would help you to fix this message in your mind.

Request advice in a confident way

Rather than asking questions that call for definite direction, such as: 'What do you think I should do?' or 'If you were in my shoes, would you . . . ?', say something like: 'I am trying to make a decision about what to do. It would really help to talk through the options I have thought of and also consider any other ideas you may have.'

Politely deflect direct advice-givers

When you hear, 'You should . . . ' or 'You must . . . ' be ready to gently raise your hand to indicate that you would like the advice-giver to stop. The earlier you can do this the better, but you may have to wait for a natural pause to emerge. Then say something like: 'Thanks so much for your concern. That's *probably* good advice, but I really do need to think this through myself. I must be clear in my mind which is the right response/action/priority for me.'

Please note the use of '*probably*.' You are not saying that their advice *is* good. You are only suggesting that it could be. Doing this preserves your right to disagree and not take their advice, but in such a way that the person doesn't feel rejected. If he or she persists in telling you what to do, then beware; they may have an over-controlling streak in their personality. Other phrases that you can use to achieve the same effect are: 'That is a possible way forward'; 'That could be a good idea'; 'You might be right'; 'Perhaps so'; 'There could be some truth in that view.'

Say an assertive, but polite, 'No' to unnecessary offers of help

Should someone say, 'I'll give them a ring for you,' respond with: 'Thanks so much for the offer, but I will ring myself.' If the helper is pleased, rather than offended by your response, you will know that they are just the kind of person you need right now. Tell them you are trying to be more self-reliant and ask them to help you achieve this goal.

View mistakes as opportunities to become braver

> *Take chances, make mistakes. That's how you grow. Pain nourishes your courage. You have to fail in order to practise being brave.*
> **Mary Tyler Moore, actress and producer**

Fear of 'getting it wrong' is one the main things that holds people back from becoming more self-reliant – staying overly dependent on others is a way of avoiding responsibility for any possible negative outcome.

Give voice to your values

> *If your morals make you dreary, depend upon it, they are wrong.*
> **Robert Louis Stevenson, nineteenth-century writer and poet**

Self-respect is crucial for psychological health. It is not possible to have genuine self-esteem or self-belief without it. In addition to loving and taking excellent care of yourself, you need to be able to look in the mirror and see someone whom you can also truly respect.

But how is self-respect achieved?

Unfortunately, most of us learn about respect the hard way. A decisive moral awakening for me came from one of my daughters when she was just eleven. I shall never forget the stinging retort she gave me in response to a demand for more respect: 'Respect has to be earned, Mother!' Although at the time this felt like a cheeky 'below-the-belt' blow, on later reflection I could see that it was well deserved. Its wisdom still impacts upon my conscience today, and it resounds in my head whenever I need reminding that, just like the respect we have for anyone else, self-respect has to be built on living proof. It isn't enough to believe in certain moral standards; you must know that you are living by them. This means that when you reflect on your behaviour, your decision-making and your lifestyle, you must be able to see the proof that your actions have been truly in sync with principles you value. Good intentions do not bring self-respect. Anyone who has felt the shame that comes with repeating the same resolution with each new year knows this well enough.

Difficult times frequently confront you with what you really value in life. They are renowned for their ability to act as a 'wake-up call'. Although no fallible human can ever maintain moral perfection, true self-respect is only possible if you are convinced that you are doing your very best to live up to your principles.

The best tip for living in line with your own principles is to compile a list of simple life rules. These can then be used as an ever-ready checklist whenever you are confronted by any kind of dilemma. As an example, I've shared three of my own below. These life rules have been immensely valuable for me. They work because they were especially created with my particular needs and bad habits in mind – see the comments in brackets. Your life rules would need to be similarly tailored especially for you.

My life rules are:

* to ask myself regularly if I am being true to my real self and my own values (I spent too many years trying to be someone I thought others wanted me to be)

* to spend more time than I think I can afford on relationships that matter most to me (I used to find it hard to say no to anyone who asked for my help, friendship or time; the result was that my close relationships suffered and I was getting burnt out)

* to see the positive in change, however unwelcome it may be (my programmed auto-response to change is depression, even though I have an excellent record of adjustment).

Try creating similar rules for yourself, but remember the following:

* They should feel **uplifting rather than burdensome**. To be motivating, they must bring you more pleasure than pain, so abiding by them should not feel in any way punishing! This is important because so often there has been an early childhood association between morality and punishment which is etched deep into the neural system. (So remember the wise words of Robert Louis Stevenson quoted at the start of this tip.)

* They should be **relevant**. They need to fit with your *current* needs and priorities. This means they will need to be reviewed and possibly changed during or after each life transition or big experience. Most parents, for

example, feel that they have to modify their guiding principles once their children come along. Other people say that they have to do this when they reach positions of leadership when it may be more appropriate to take a more conciliatory stance on many issues. During difficult times, you often have to be more compromising than you would otherwise be and this prompts a review of your principles.

* They should be **defendable**. They have to be able to stand up to the rigour of a 'devil's advocate' test. You can do this for yourself, but you will have even more confidence in your principles if you can test them out with other people. To do the test on your own, use a two-chair exercise, whereby you start by sitting on one chair and making your case for your belief in one rule, then sit in the chair opposite you and take the stance of someone who believes the opposite. To do the test with someone else, ask a friend to take the role of devil's advocate or, if you are brave, you could start a debate with someone you know who you think truly does have opposite views from you.

* They should be **publishable**. In other words, they should not give you any cause for embarrassment. They need to reflect values that you are proud to be seen to uphold. If they do not, they will deplete rather than enhance your self-respect and self-belief.

Another way of putting your life rules through a rigorous test is to read books or articles on the Internet which express different views from yours.

Most people find that between three and six guiding life rules listed in hierarchical order is ideal – few enough to commit to memory, but enough to cover the key moral issues that will confront you. If you find it a struggle to come up with a list (and many people do at first attempt) this simple exercise will help you to clarify your key values.

Your personal heroes

1. Make a list of about ten people you admire. These can be: people in your own personal life, such as family, friends or colleagues; famous people, dead or alive; fictional characters from books, films, TV or computer games.

2. Make notes on what it is or was about their behaviour, their lifestyle and their achievements that you admire.

3. Beside each name put down three to six value adjectives that you would associate with them as in the examples below:

   * Nelson Mandela – courageous, persistent, flexible, visionary, humble
   * Florence Nightingale – kind, persistent, pioneering, humble
   * Superman – helpful, unusual, strong, ordinary at heart
   * Grandmother – tolerant, modest, hard-working, resilient

When you have finished, see if you notice any similarities in these people and the way they lead/led their lives (imaginary or otherwise); usually, people find some

QUICK FIX: Stifle your selfish survival response with good deeds

Dousing the Protectionism Flames
Newspaper headline during the global financial crisis, 2009

Twenty leaders from different countries gathered in London on the day of this news story. Their aim was to find ways of collaborating in order to solve the world's economic problems, as it was clear that 'protectionism' (i.e. national selfishness) is one of the greatest obstacles to achieving this goal.

In difficult times, most people naturally prioritise looking after their own, but in the long term, there is a hefty price to be paid for this 'survival-of-the-fittest' impulse. Your self-respect will plummet and your relationships with your community will deteriorate.

One way to guard against this happening is to make it a rule for yourself to do one good deed each day, and record your act of kindness in a small notebook or in a file on your computer. You may not keep to your rule each day, but the monitoring process will prevent any selfish protectionist trend from getting its grip on you.

Your record can also serve as a more general self-esteem-boosting resource. Look at it whenever you need a reminder that you are actually 'nice' occasionally!

even if there is not a repetition of the exact words. So, using the example above, the themes that emerge could be: being of service to others, resilient in the face of problems and confident and successful but not arrogant.

By this stage of the exercise, you should be starting to get ideas about the life rules you might want to make for yourself. If you still need some help, try doing the exercise with a friend. This should help you both to clarify your values especially if you play the devil's advocate game (see p. 58).

4. Finally, you need to put your rules through some real-life tests. When you are faced with your next dilemma, use them as a reference guide. If they feel helpful and bring results that give you a sense of pride, they are right for you. If they fail this test, don't give up; it may take time to find a set that works for you.

> *It has taken thirty-three years and a bang on the head to get my values right.*
> **Sir Stirling Moss, world champion racing driver**

 ## Get a grip on your guilt

> *Every man is guilty of all the good he didn't do.*
> **Voltaire, writer and philosopher**

My own struggle to live with this tricky emotion started very young. I was brought up in convents which was tough on an adventurous child who found sinning very exciting.

But I became cunning and was rarely found out. I largely avoided the cruel caning that so many of my friends endured, but my punishment lasted longer. It came in the form of persistent internal guilt. This feeling gnawed away at my self-esteem and was partly responsible for much of the self-destructive behaviour that nearly destroyed my life in early adulthood.

So not surprisingly, when I later become a psychotherapist, I developed a special interest in this topic. Almost every client I have ever had has been troubled in some way by guilt. I have seen it sabotage the efforts of many able people when they are in the midst of difficulties. They plague themselves with obsessive self-questioning and self-blame, tending to feel overly responsible for their problems.

Dealing with guilt

Key 1: Stop wishing your guilt away

Accept that, unless you are a psychopath without a conscience, guilt is going to be one of life's companions! As is the case with any irritating 'companion' you are stuck with, it is your responsibility to find a way of managing the relationship. No magic wand can make it disappear.

Key 2: Label guilt as 'True' or 'False'

True guilt is when you know you have done something which is not in line with your own moral code. This kind of feeling is a positive force. Its function is to produce enough discomfort to prompt you back on to the straight and narrow. It also curtails arrogance, and psychologists believe that it evolved in order to enable us to work co-operatively in groups as our tasks and problems were becoming more complex and too challenging for one individual.

False guilt is the kind you may feel even when your intellect and moral code tell you that you have done no wrong. This kind of feeling is usually triggered by someone else's real or imagined disapproval. A classic example for women today is when they feel guilty for leaving their children in the care of someone else to go out to work, while for men, it is when they feel guilty because they have had to accept sustenance from someone else because they have no means to feed, clothe or educate their family. In both cases, such 'guilt trips' are often linked to values which were absorbed at an impressionable age from parents or grandparents or the more general influence of a culture or religion.

False guilt can also be an irrational symptom of people in a state of grief or depression. An example of this would be the 'survivor guilt' felt by many Jews after the Holocaust or by families of people who have died in an accident or disaster. Another example of false guilt emerging in difficult times is when a recession causes a sharp rise in redundancies. Those who have managed to keep their jobs while so many around them have lost theirs are sometimes plagued by guilt.

Both true and false guilt can have debilitating and demotivating effects, and as they often feel the same, even very bright, self-aware people may confuse the two. Correct labelling of the emotion is essential because the action we need to take for each kind is different. You may need help to do this from someone you can trust to be objective and honest.

Key 3: Take appropriate action
Action for true guilt
Say sorry and spell out what you have learnt and intend to do differently as a result. Make recompense in the best way you can. For example, you may not be able to undo what you said or did, but you could send flowers, do a good turn or send a donation to an appropriate charity. Give yourself a self-esteem boost (see Mini-boosts, pp. 40–2).

Action for false guilt
Identify the cause of the false guilt. Read the tip about perfectionism (pp. 68–71) and remind yourself of your own guiding moral code and life priorities (see pp. 55–61).

Next, compose a 'permission' sentence that counters the unwanted moral message in your subconscious mind. It should remind you of one of your own good moral traits and a basic human right. For example, 'I strive to be a good parent and have a right to make my own mind up about the wrong and right way to bring up my children.' Or, 'I am a compassionate and generous person even if I am exercising my right to work/be happy/live when others cannot.' Write your sentence out again twenty times, then, with a calm, firm voice, read it aloud. This may sound boring and punitive, but it does work. Repetition is the key to programming moral directives into your mind. But in this exercise, you are in the director's chair. Each time you feel your false guilt resurface repeat your sentence several times in your head.

If your false guilt remains persistent it may mean that it relates to an unhealed emotional wound, in the way that the survivor guilt mentioned above does. The answer then is to see a therapist or counsellor or read my self-help book, *The Emotional Healing Strategy* (see Resources, p. 265).

 ## Ask for compliments even when you know you have done well

A temporary swallowing of your humility is required while you read this tip, something that could be quite a challenge for British readers! Being bad at receiving compliments is just one of those habits that takes time and effort to break. It was deeply entrenched in my personality for the first thirty years of my life, but I'm I am proud to say that there is not a trace of it left. I feel only pure pleasure now when someone tells me that I have done well or that I am looking good.

So how did I achieve this transformation? It was sheer persistence with the advice I was given in assertiveness training. Firstly, I gave myself endless practice at just listening attentively to the compliments, allowing them to be absorbed and then replying with a simple, 'Thank you'. Then, when I found that this response didn't leave me friendless, I began to add an extra sentence of self-appreciation, such as, 'Yes, I was pleased with the way I did that – I felt it was quite an achievement.'

After a few weeks of practice, I found that I could take the super-assertive step of asking for a clarifying expansion of the compliment, for example: 'What was it about the way I did it that you thought worked well?'

And finally, I reached the peak of compliment-gathering. I started to take the big risk and proactively 'fish' for compliments even when I felt I didn't need them because I was certain I had done well. For example, after giving a talk that I can tell has gone down well with the audience, I might say to the organiser: 'I feel pleased with the way that went, but I'd really like to know what you think.' The vast majority of the time, the answer is one that will fluff up my feathers a little more, but I may get some negative feedback as well. This, of course, can be useful, and I probably would never hear it if I didn't asked for others' opinions.

This particular personal development journey has been one of the hardest I have ever had to take, but the rewards have made it worth it. Try taking the steps I've just described if you struggle to allow compliments to soak into your self-esteem. Compliments will help to immunise you against wounds to your pride and build self-confidence. And we all need many more of them during difficult times. You should never be embarrassed about taking or asking for them. And, of course, you should take care not to forget to give them out freely, even to people who appear not to need them.

QUICK FIX: Welcome the wisdom you are gaining

A single conversation with a wise man is better than ten years of study.
Chinese proverb

Whenever you feel your confidence is rocky and you are not sure whether you can take (or even survive!) the next step, do the following:

* Recall the last failure, semi-failure or hurtful experience you had. Think of at least one thing you learnt as a result, for example: that your strengths are not organisational and you are better at nurturing people; that there isn't a market for . . . and that potential customers asked for more . . . ; that not everyone likes a hug when they cry.

* Think of one piece of wisdom you could gain from having to live through a potentially daunting experience. For example, perhaps your current problem is an enforced career change, living on your own or a drop in your standard of living. Although you may prefer not to have to face this kind of challenge, highlighting a potential gain in wisdom could help you to approach it a little more positively.

Go for 'good enough'

Striving for excellence motivates you; striving for perfection is demoralising.
Harriet Braiker, psychologist and author

The chances are that if you are reading this book, you have a tendency to be a perfectionist. I am making this guess because the majority of my clients during the past thirty years who have been struggling through tough times have had this characteristic.

To see if I've guessed right, look at the following statements and tick the boxes that could apply to you, most of the time. You tend to:

❑ set goals and standards for yourself that are so high that they become a strain on your time, energy or money and some of your relationships.

❑ find it hard to take a compliment without either doubting the giver's sincerity or their ability as a true judge, or thinking or commenting on some aspect that could be improved.

❑ dwell on mistakes and failures for longer than most people and are not at ease when others try to comfort or cheer you up.

❑ feel you could or should have done better, even though people are continually telling you that you have done well or you know your results are better than the average.

❑ believe that aiming for perfection is the key to success and should always be your goal.

❏ hate deadlines and wait until the very last minute to make decisions or hand in work so you have the option to make any last-minute changes.

❏ have packed schedules and less relaxation than most people.

❏ become irritated or angered by others who do things which are not up to your standards, even when it is not your responsibility to judge or supervise them.

❏ focus more on your own and others' weaknesses rather than strengths.

❏ have at least one self-improvement project on the go and more in the pipeline; if not, you feel guilty.

The higher your score out of ten, the more of a perfectionist you are. And if you are now questioning the validity of this simple assessment, you can add another three ticks to your score and read on! If your score was very low, however, I would urge you to read on in any case, as this will give you an idea of how to help others who have this trait.

And now the confession! I am a perfectionist myself and highly attracted to other perfectionists and perfect creations. So I have great empathy for you. But I also know that during tough times this is something that can render you more vulnerable to stress, being burnt out, pessimistic and feeling isolated and unsupported.

I am not going to suggest that you give up your perfectionism completely though! You need to simply tame it, especially in difficult times. The exercise overleaf will give you a checklist that you can refer to whenever necessary to ensure that you stay on a good-enough track most of the time. I assure you that doing this will free up considerable time, energy and possibly money. It will also make it much easier for you to collaborate with anyone who is helping you.

QUICK FIX: View the big picture of your potential

Imagine that you are eighty years old. A large group of friends and ex-colleagues are throwing a party for you. Someone has been asked to write a speech about you, your achievements and why you have been and still are such an inspiration to others. What would fill your heart with pleasure and pride to hear in this speech? Use your imagination liberally to answer this question and make notes accordingly. Keep these notes somewhere you can see them (and perhaps add to them) regularly.

> *People who are constantly looking at the whole picture have the best chance of succeeding in any endeavour.*
> **John Maxwell, leadership and personal development guru**

Perfectionism exercise

The aim of this exercise is to categorise your activities in relation to the standard you need to achieve. You will reserve 'Gold star' standards in a few special areas of your life. The rest will be relegated to 'Silver' and 'Bronze'. When you meet new circumstances you may need to do some rearranging. But always make sure that if you add something to your Gold list, you downgrade something else to Silver or Bronze.

On a piece of paper or suitable computer programme, draw three columns with the headings Gold, Silver and Bronze. Enter each activity into one of the three columns. Next, enter your main everyday tasks into one of the columns. Below is an example of how I did this for some of my own activities.

Gold	*Silver*	*Bronze*
Work	*Work*	*Work*
Writing books	Writing articles	Writing emails
Clients with a pressing problem	Interviews with journalists	Updating website
	Currently OK clients	Networking
	Talks	General office admin
Personal	*Personal*	*Personal*
Supporting my daughter	Health maintenance	House maintenance
Quality time with husband	Close friends	Other pastimes
Health crises	Reading novels	

Always live up to your standards – by lowering them, if necessary.

Mignon McLaughlin, author of *The Second Neurotic's Notebook*

SECTION 3
Manage Your Moods

People often think that you are born either a moody person or not, the assumption being that those who can stay cool and calm during difficult times are genetically privileged, while others will always be at the mercy of their moods and therefore have a harder time. The tips in this section should help to dispel this myth.

Emotional intelligence – a person's ability to understand their own (and others') emotions and to use them appropriately – is something that can be learnt by absolutely anyone, although it may take some a little longer to develop it than others; just how long will depend partly on your inherited temperament, as well as the amount of time you invest in finding out what does or does not work for you as an individual. This is partly why this section is the longest in the book – I wanted to include tips to suit all kinds of emotional predispositions, and the only way to know whether or not they will work for you is to try a range of them out.

The other reason why this section is the longest is because difficult times tend to generate a greater degree of feeling than normal, making them testing times even for those who usually manage their moods well. So you may well find that while your favourite ways of calming yourself down are not quite good enough in tough times, there are some new ideas here for you to try that will help you.

Constantly check whether it's you or your autopilot that is in control

Temperament lies behind mood; behind will, lies the fate of character. Then behind both, the influence of family the tyranny of culture; and finally the power of climate and environment; and we are free, only to the extent we rise above these.

John Burroughs, naturalist and essayist

Long before the birth of 'emotional intelligence' wise people knew that control over your feelings was crucial for functioning well and being happy. Especially during hard times, you need to be fully aware of the kind of circumstances which might flip you out of control and into autopilot mode. When this happens, your head is out of a job. It is your feelings that are in the driving seat and you have no choice but to dance to a tune composed partly by your primitive 'animal' self and partly by a set of neural connections which were haphazardly created through a combination of nature and nurture.

Although it is commonly said that the 'true self' comes out when you lose your cool or are challenged by fear, in my opinion this is nonsense. Our emotional autopilots were, after all, hard-wired without our conscious consent. I know mine certainly was. When, for example, my emotional autopilot is in control, it makes an appalling mess of my life. This is because my original mental programming triggered a muddle of contradictory responses. This is not surprising – my parents' bitter and tragic personal war combined with the external pressures of the Second World War and the constant traumas of life in a succession of care homes programmed my auto-pilot to always act as though a major catastrophe is about to hit. This is why I remain alert to the possibility that, in certain circumstances, I will overreact and start to produce a package of confusing yo-yo behaviours that were 'designed' *for* me, not *by* me. The job description of my autopilot is to deal with the threatened survival of a powerless child, not a confident and capable grown-up psychotherapist!

I am aware that my autopilot programming was not 'normal'. But I also know that there are many people whose autopilot is even less well equipped to deal with their real adult world. And, even if your nature and nurture were 'blessed', they can't have been perfect. So we all need to take care when we enter into the danger zones which trip us into auto-emotional mode. Your feelings, whether they are good or bad, are not necessarily 'the real you'.

Difficult times tend to bring many of the circumstances that constitute an emotional danger zone into play. Your autopilot is likely to jump into the driving seat when you:

* are tired or physically weak due to illness or in pain

* are facing something that makes you frightened or very anxious

* think that you have been treated unfairly and are angry

* feel helpless and think you have no power to change the situation

* encounter someone or a situation that has echoes of a significant person or event in your past

* are in a highly excitable state – perhaps due to being 'in love' or because you have an idea or project that you care 'passionately' about.

Can you relate to any of the above right now? If not, you are lucky and should be prepared for your good fortune on this account to change. It can happen to literally anyone if they are put under enough pressure.

When you know you are in 'at-risk' circumstances, ask yourself the following three questions:

1. Is what I am doing or saying appropriate for the here-and-now situation?

2. Is this feeling similar to one that I felt very deeply in the past?

3. Is this idea really a good intuition or simply a fear or irritation or attraction that has resurfaced from the past because my brain has encountered a reminder?

If you answer 'No' to question 1, stop what you are doing as soon as possible. After taking some time out to de-stress your body, take time for a rethink.

If you answer 'Yes' to questions 2 or 3, don't skip the next tip!

If you answer 'Yes' to the first question, and 'No' to the other two – again, continue reading. Firstly, it will help you to help others who may need support from your emotional strength. Secondly, you will at least be well prepared should your own circumstances become rocky one day.

> *The most courageous decision you make each day is the decision to be in a good mood.*
> **Voltaire, French writer and philosopher**

QUICK FIX: Rebalance your pulse with slow repetitive rhythm

Repetitive rhythms such as drumming, bell ringing or Gregorian chants have been used for centuries as calming devices. Today, contemporary relaxation specialists will use a wide variety of rhythmic sounds, such as recordings of natural rhythmic phenomena like lapping waves or specially composed electronic pieces, using steady beats that are heard by the subconscious mind.

You can create a good-enough effect instantly though, without any fancy musical equipment. When you feel your heart beating faster, just slow your pulse by closing your eyes and tapping your fingers or a pencil in a slow rhythmic way on something hard. If your attention wanders away back to your worries, take a couple of deep, slow breaths from the depths of your stomach and focus back on the sound of your tapping. Trust that your pulse will slow and it will.

Grade your feeling

If you are having an uncomfortable feeling, give the degree of emotion you are experiencing a grade. Use something that has, or could trigger in you, the greatest degree of that feeling. For example, on a scale of one to ten:

Sadness

10   Death of a partner or child
3   Loss of a potential job you'd hoped to get

Fear

10   Being on the front line in a war
1   Having an operation that is performed daily all over the world

This mini-strategy works because it makes you switch into analytical thinking mode, automatically reducing the degree of your feeling and helping you to feel more in control.

 # Get a handle on your 'hard drive'

It's terrible – I can hear my mother's voice coming out of my own mouth! You know how I always swore I'd never be like her, but nowadays I'm irritable all the time. The kids' quarrelling just

gets to me and I start saying the kind of things she used to say to us. I feel so ashamed. Last week, I even heard myself say, 'If this carries on, I'll be back in hospital and then you'll be sorry!' I think I've gone right back to square one. I feel such a failure. Just when I think I've cracked it, life gives me another whack. I know you'll probably say – like everyone else – that I should be positive, but there's no fight left in me. Remember, my mother was only four years older than I am now when she died – you can't fight your genes.

Carol, a breast cancer sufferer and mother of boys aged five and eight

Being a good parent was at the top of Carol's list of life goals when she first came to see me a few years ago. She went to a number of drama therapy weekends that I run and worked very successfully on developing her self-confidence. She used to be very quiet and unassuming, but for years had been managing well without any help: she had reached a senior management position at work, had a happy marriage, a new circle of close friends and had also become an excellent parent. Indeed, all was going as well as any of us can expect from life until three years ago. This was when Carol was diagnosed with breast cancer. Her initial treatment went well and her prognosis appeared to be good, but then another lump appeared. This time she was advised to have a mastectomy.

Bad as this health problem was, it did not seem to me to be enough to throw the 'new' Carol so off course. So, I questioned her further. She then revealed that she had very strong suspicions that her husband was having an affair. He denied it, but she knew that their relationship had 'not been the same' since the most recent breast crisis, and she now feared that this mastectomy would finally finish it. Worse still, she had a scenario running through her head that she could die soon and the boys would lose both parents if her husband had left.

With the shock and multiple stresses of her current life, Carol's 'hard drive' (or autopilot) had taken control of her thinking and many of her responses. Because I knew about Carol's background, I could very quickly spot what was going on. I knew that reassuring comfort and problem-solving strategies would, at that moment, fall on deaf ears. Before she could use the resources of her intelligent mind and her supportive friends, she needed to get back in the driving seat of her own brain.

For those of us who are used to helping people through crises, there is nothing unusual about this situation. It can happen to any of us and, like Carol, we might not be aware of what is happening. It often takes confrontation from someone else who is both knowledgeable and assertive to make us realise that we are not in full control of our conscious thinking mind and our feelings. For Carol, it was a good friend who persuaded her to go back to me. As it happens, this was good for Carol because she had gone beyond the stage where she could pull herself out of her depressed rut. But the good news is that it didn't take long to do this together, mainly because Carol already had so much self-awareness. She has now had her mastectomy and is considering reconstructive surgery. Her husband has agreed to couple counselling and I understand it is going well. Her friends organised a 'babysitting rota' among themselves so that she has a break from the children twice a week. Her strength is returning day by day and she has negotiated with her employer that she can start back on flexi-time for the first six months. 'New' Carol is well and truly back in charge!

To ensure that she keeps a handle on the negative ideas and responses on her hard drive, Carol did the following exercise with me. I have used extracts from hers as examples. Try it for yourself. (If you, like Carol, had what might be termed as 'a very difficult childhood', you may need a few sessions with a therapist as well to help you achieve enough insight.)

Carol's hard drive reminder exercise

Negative response	Examples	Derivation
Philosophising	Blood is thicker than water	Mum's fantasy
Self-talk	'You idiot'; 'You never learn'	Teacher's lack of faith
Feelings	Fear of change	No practice or role models as a child
Reactions to people	Submissive to authority	Repressive schooling; caning
Mind-reading	He must think I am . . .	Outsider as child/ low self-esteem
Gloomy predictions	Knowing my luck . . .	Series of bad-luck experiences; early failures

Negative response	*Examples*	*Derivation*
Behaviour	Withdrawal; not speaking up; not asking for help	Dad; punishment
Words/phrases	Shut up; You never listen; Do as I tell you	School and Dad

Make a list of the key examples you came up with and keep it to hand as a warning. Look at it from time to time while you are going through a difficult period. And remember that they will surface when you are stressed. So first, you need to relax and recover, then pick up this book again to help you find something that will quickly reboot your morale and get you back into positive problem-solving mode.

 ## Know what to sniff and smell

You may break, you may shatter the vase,
if you will,
But the scent of the roses will hang around still.
Thomas More, Renaissance scholar and statesman

I love this quote – the reminder that even when life (the vase) has been shattered, the memories and good feelings of its beautiful moments (the roses) will remain and can still be evoked.

We can also add scientific understanding to the wisdom behind Thomas More's poetic philosophising. We now know that the response centre for smell is located in the most primitive region of the emotional brain where memories are stored. This is why scents always evoke an instant feeling response and will, more often than not, evoke memories as well.

When I return home from a spell in our house in Spain, I often find it hard to settle back in to my London life, especially on a dark, gloomy day. Once, when I was feeling stressed at the thought of a few weeks of being chained to my computer, I decided to go out and buy some jasmine oil. Burning this immediately uplifted my mood; it recreated the pleasurable, relaxed sensation that I feel when the scent of the jasmine wafts through our Spanish home.

Try using this primitive mechanism whenever you need a quick emotional lift. Choose a scent that you once associated with happier times. If there isn't oil to burn or a scent to spray, you can simply use your imagination. By recalling your memory and concentrating on recreating the aromas in your mind, you make your body produce the good feelings associated with those positive memories. If you find this hard to believe, just close your eyes and imagine you are squeezing a lemon and then starting to drink the juice. You will find your body instantly reacting. Now practise recreating the pleasurable sensations evoked by these scents:

* Fresh-cut summer grass

* Sea air

* A bowl of fresh rose petals

* Your favourite scent

* Your favourite meal

QUICK FIX: Top and tail each day with treats

The start and end of your day can often create a 'downer' effect: this is when you are alone with your thoughts – when the stark reality of a problem or feelings of aloneness often loom largest. So it's easy to get into the habit of worrying the moment you wake up or when you switch off the light at night, especially if your day is so busy that you fall into bed too late at night, set the alarm for the latest time you can wake up, giving yourself a tense and rushed start to the day.

After one great de-stressing holiday, I realised that there was no reason why I could not do at home one of the things I'd enjoyed most on holiday – reading in bed. I just had to make waking and going to bed earlier a new ritual. I did that, and haven't looked back for eighteen years!

Choose one or more enjoyable activities that you can easily do and that will have the same effect.

Get prepared for panic paralysis

Anxiety is a bully – it takes from your life, and every concession you make to it, it takes more. It will never be enough.

Catherine O'Neill, Awareness Manager at Anxiety UK

If you are prone to anxiety, difficult periods might provoke a panic attack. If you have never had one before and don't recognise the symptoms and how to deal with them, they can be very frightening. So frightening that you become anxious about having another attack, and so then, of course, you do!

Symptoms, which tend to occur very suddenly, without any warning and often for no apparent reason, include:

* the sensation that your heart is beating irregularly (palpitations)
* the sensation of being detached from the world around you (depersonalisation)
* sweating
* trembling
* hot flushes
* chills
* shortness of breath
* choking sensation
* chest pain
* nausea
* dizziness
* feeling faint
* numbness or pins and needles
* dry mouth
* a need to go to the toilet
* ringing in your ears.

Because the symptoms are often very intense, you may feel like you are having a heart attack or, worse still, dying. The fear of having a heart attack can then add to your sense of panic. If you need more convincing that every single one of these symptoms is consistent with an anxiety attack, consult your doctor or a reputable health information website.

The following strategy is based on the advice of Anxiety UK (see Resources, p. 265), a leading charity that is dedicated to helping people with anxiety disorders.

Strategy for dealing with a panic attack

Step 1: Reassure yourself with the facts

Use informed self-talk to quell the thoughts that have been produced by your feelings of fear. Here are some statements you could use that will counteract the most common fears:

* *This is not dangerous.* Because if this was a heart attack your symptoms would not reduce if you slowed down your breathing, sat down or left the situation, as they often do when you are having a panic attack. All your other symptoms are normal physiological reactions during an attack of anxiety.

* *I am not going to collapse.* Because your blood pressure increases when you experience anxiety, making you less likely to faint.

* *I can cope.* Because you have a strategy and you are in control.

* *I don't need to run away.* Because you will gain control and if you run away the panic attack wins and will go on

winning. People can and do carry on with highly respon-sible jobs while experiencing and controlling these symptoms. Nobody except you is likely to notice that you are having an anxiety attack.

* *Panic attacks pass.* Because no one can sustain a panic attack for ever – usually they do not last for longer than an hour.

Step 2: Slow down your breathing

Take control of your breathing by doing the following exercise. Repeat until you feel your breathing has returned to normal.

1. Breathe in deeply from your diaphragm (count to 6)

2. Rest (count to 2)

3. Breathe out slowly (count to 12)

4. Rest (count to 2)

Step 3: Engage yourself in a distracting activity

To stabilise your breathing and take your mind off your attack, do something that distracts your attention away from your body. This could, for example, be work, a cross-word, simply counting backwards from fifty or how many objects of a certain colour there are around you.

Step 4: Review your lifestyle

Check that you are giving yourself enough time to de-stress your mind and your body on a regular basis throughout the day. Almost all the tips in the first five sections of this book can help you to do this. But don't overwhelm yourself with different goals (a common mistake of anxious people); choose a few ideas that you think could particularly help you at the moment and make an action plan to help you to integrate them into your life.

Practise this strategy regularly and use it whenever you become aware of minor anxiety symptoms such as fluttering feelings in your stomach. If you do then have a panic attack, you will know the routine and apply it almost automatically.

Make a mood music compilation

Music has a direct fast link to the emotional centre of the brain, especially if the music is associated with events in the past which evoked powerful feelings. Listening to that music immediately recreates the same emotions felt when that memory was recorded.

So why not make yourself some personal compilations of music that will, for example, bring back positive feelings to help you deal with today's challenges? Here are five different ideas for compilations that I'd find useful during difficult times:

* **For excitement (especially with just life itself)** – Scott Joplin ragtime music, because it recreates the memory of my first baby daughter dancing delightedly in her baby bouncer.

* **For carefree gaiety** – Sevillana flamenco music, because it brings back the joyful memories of seeing people of all ages and abilities dancing joyously together at ferias.

* **For optimism** – Elvis Presley's 'Blue Suede Shoes', because it brings back memories of secretive listening to pirate radio in my teen years, when I felt sure that a positive change in my life and the world was possible.

* **For confidence** – the march from Verdi's *Aida*, because I listened to it on the way to a very successful talk I gave for a big, daunting audience.

* **For calm contentment** – the adagio of Mahler's 5th symphony, because it reminds me of the treasured companionship of my husband who also loves this music.

Once you have made your own personal compilations, keep them handy, so that you can use them to change your feeling state whenever you need to.

 # Feed a positive mood

The UK Mental Health Foundation recommends boosting your intake of certain nutrients to target common mood problems, as follows:

Problem	*Nutrients*
Anxiety	Folic acid and magnesium
Poor concentration	Vitamin B_1

QUICK FIX: Write away your worries

> *Worry does not empty tomorrow of its sorrow;*
> *it empties today of its strength.*
> **Corrie ten Boom, campaigner and writer**

Corrie ten Boom joined the Dutch underground movement during the Nazi occupation in the Second World War. When it was discovered that she was hiding Jews, she and her family were sent to prison and concentration camps. She survived only because she was released as a result of a clerical error. Most of her family died in the camps. She spent much of the rest of her life writing books and articles and doing rehabilitation work with survivors of prison experiences all over the world.

A tried-and-tested way to deal with worries is to get them out of your head and on to paper. Keep a little book to jot them down in and ensure you have it with you as much of the time as possible. When choosing your book, try to find one that has pages which can be easily torn out. You can then do a monthly review and rip out the pages with worries that are no longer a big issue for you. You will be surprised at how quickly your book disappears!

Problem	*Nutrients*
Depression	Vitamins B_3, B_6 and C, folic acid, magnesium, selenium, zinc, omega 3 fatty acids, tryptophan, tyrosine and GABA
Irritability	Vitamin B_6, magnesium, selenium

Look at the areas you need to boost, then find at least one or two key foods from the list below that will address these and add them to your shopping list!

Foods that will provide the required nutrients

Nutrient	*Food*
Folic acid	Green leafy vegetables, calf liver and turkey, cod, salmon, halibut, shrimp, sesame seeds, hazelnuts and cashew nuts, walnuts, most beans and pulses, oranges
Vitamin B_1	Wholegrain/brown bread, oats, rice, barley, pasta, lentils, peppers, cabbage, broccoli, asparagus, lettuce, mushrooms, spinach, watercress, green peas, aubergine, sunflower seeds, Brazil nuts, hazelnuts, pecans, pine nuts, pistachios, sesame seeds, tuna, salmon, mussels, pork
Vitamin B_3	Brown rice, rice bran, wheatgerm, broccoli, mushrooms, cabbage, sprouts, courgette, squash, peanuts, beef liver and kidneys, pork, turkey, chicken, tuna, salmon, sunflower seeds

Nutrient	*Food*
Vitamin B$_6$	Brown rice, oats, bran, barley, bananas, mango, tuna, trout, salmon, avocados, watercress, cauliflower, cabbage, peppers, squash, asparagus, pak choi, potatoes, chicken, pork, turkey, lima beans, soya beans, chick peas, sunflower seeds
Vitamin C	Red peppers, red cabbage, broccoli, sprouts, cauliflower, strawberries, oranges, tangerines, kiwi, cranberries, pineapple
Magnesium	Spinach, watercress, avocados, peppers, broccoli, green cabbage, almonds, Brazil nuts, cashews, peanuts, macadamias, walnuts, pecans, pumpkin, sunflower seeds, poppy seeds, oatmeal, buckwheat, barley, quinoa, plain yoghurt, baked beans, bananas, kiwi, blackberries, strawberries, oranges, raisins
Selenium	Wheat germ, brewer's yeast, calf liver, turkey breast, cod, tuna, halibut, salmon, shrimp, mushrooms, garlic, spinach, sunflower seeds, tofu, barley, rye, oats, brown long-grain rice, mozzarella cheese, mustard and sunflower seeds

In addition, drink more water, herbal and fruit infusions and pure fruit juices. Not drinking enough fluid has significant implications for mental health. During an average day in the UK, an adult's body loses approximately 2.5 litres of water through the lungs as water vapour, through the skin as perspiration or through the kidneys as urine. In times of stress you lose even more water than usual from your body. If sufficient fluids (the recommended minimum is 2 litres a day) are not consumed to replace this loss, the symptoms of inadequate hydration can appear, including increased irritability, loss of concentration and reduced efficiency in mental tasks.

QUICK FIX: Heed hunger pangs

Allowing yourself to become too hungry can make you irritable, eat too quickly and get indigestion, reach out for fast foods that are fattening and not very nutritional and eat much more than you need.

Avoid these unnecessary knocks to your self-esteem and physical wellbeing by heeding your hunger pangs at an early stage. Always have a nutritious snack to hand. You may need more of these because your normal meal schedule is likely to be interrupted in difficult times.

Use mindfulness to quell strong emotion

Mindfulness is the name that has been given to a certain style of quick and easy meditation techniques. The essence of all of the different types that now exist is that you focus your mind on what is happening at present, either within you or around you.

Don't get too boiling – a simple strategy for defusing irritation

This strategy should be used as soon as you notice you are becoming irritated. It will send 'switch-off' signals to the primitive emergency 'fight/flight/freeze' response centre in your emotional brain. It can be done very rapidly and discreetly if you are with people.

Don't	Get	Too	Boiling
I	R	E	R
S	O	N	E
T	U	S	A
A	N	I	T
N	D	O	H
C		N	E
E			

Distance

Commonly, people grip or squeeze something when they are frustrated or angry; so let go of any tight physical contact. Take a step back or lean back in your chair, leave the room or 'sleep on it' as Grandma might have advised!

Ground

If your anger response has gone into 'fight' mode, you will probably now want to move around to get ready for action. You can steady yourself by putting both feet firmly uncrossed on the ground or lightly balancing yourself against an object or surface, such as a chair or wall. Then bring yourself back down to earth by switching your brain into thinking mode: try something like counting all the blue objects in the room, the number of circles you can see or counting backwards from fifty.

Tension

Release the tension out of your body by doing one or more muscle relaxers:

* Clenching and unclenching your fists

* Screwing up your face and releasing muscles slowly

* Curling and uncurling toes

* Thumping or kicking a cushion

* Shaking your wrists

Breathe

Do the following (or another) breathing exercise to ensure that your pulse is slowed down:

* Take deep breaths in from the bottom of your stomach to the count of 3.

* Hold for a count of 2.

* Release your breath slowly to the count of 6.

Neuroscientific research has shown that mindfulness meditations, such as the one I suggest below, actually do make noticeable changes in the brain's structure as well as in its activity. Findings suggest that there is a thickening in the tissue that processes emotion. But there is yet another benefit too, which is of interest to those of us who are approaching their senior years: the technique appears also to slow down the age-related thinning of the cortex area (where thinking is processed).

Try using the following technique whenever you feel strong emotion rising. It can be done in a matter of minutes or even in a few seconds.

1. Close your eyes for just a few seconds and focus your mind's eye on visualising the physical happenings in your body. Imagine, for example, that you can see your heart pumping away, the blood circulating around your body, your lungs moving in and out.

2. After watching this imaginary movie of your organs at work, notice how your feeling sensations lessened when you diverted your attention to your internal physical experience.

Because this technique is so very easy to use, you can quickly switch into it in everyday frustrating situations. Here are some examples of when it could be useful:

* You are driving and there is a hold-up that you know will last a long time.

* You are in a queue in a shop and the person ahead of you has an item that has no price on it. The assistant has

to ring the supervisor who appears to be on her lunch break, so someone has to call the manager who is in the car park.

* Your children are late for school. They are immersed in a quarrel about which one of them will take the only umbrella that can be found in the house. You know it will be good to let them sort the quarrel out between themselves and take the consequences of being late. This will take a few moments, so you can sit tight and use mindfulness to control your escalating irritation.

If you happen to be an artist, you might be especially interested to know that this kind of exercise not only helps you to contain strong emotion, but also helps you to become more creative. Ellen J. Langer (professor of psychology and author of *On Becoming an Artist: Reinventing Yourself Through Creativity*) has studied the effects of mindfulness: 'More than thirty years of research has shown that mindfulness is figuratively and literally enlivening. It's the way you feel when you're feeling passionate.'

Prevent molehills of irritation from growing into volcanoes of rage

For twenty-five years, Steve had had his own plumber's merchant shop in the centre of town. He had inherited the business from his father and was well known and trusted in the community. When a large national DIY chain with a plumbing section opened in a commercial park on the outskirts of town, he was confident that it would not pose a threat. For several years, his business stayed stable, but when an economic downturn began to bite into the budgets of his clients, they were forced to put aside their loyalty and go for the superstore's lower prices.

Steve had always been renowned for being cheerful and unflappable. His staff found him a generous and easy-going employer. But as his financial worries increased, he became irritated by both his staff and his family. Things like his staff popping out for 10 minutes to get their cappuccinos, lights left on, his children's skateboards lying in the hall, their music playing too loudly and his wife's chatter on the phone to her sister all began to grate on his nerves. But he'd swallow down his irritation and say nothing. Eventually though, he would snap and lose his temper over 'something and nothing'. Steve was aware of what was at the root of his outbursts, so he would apologise profusely and make even more of an effort to stay calm in the face of these petty annoyances. But he did not seem to be able to change this pattern of behaviour and his outbursts continued.

His wife persuaded him to go to his GP to ask for something to calm his nerves. The doctor instead lent him my book *Managing Anger* (see Resources, p. 265) from the surgery's library. As Steve is not a great reader, he contacted me instead. It seemed that as he had never suffered a short-fuse problem before, he just did not know how to handle the feelings that this new stressful situation had generated. The solution for him was some simple anger-management strategies. His difficult trading situation hasn't yet changed, but he has at least regained his usual emotional equilibrium and, as I write, is considering his options with the help of a small-business adviser.

It is very easy to let minor irritations build up when you have major problems to contend with. Even if you, like

QUICK FIX: Ask yourself to dance

Dancing is a wonderful way to let go of pent-up feelings and tension. And we also now know that it has benefits for the brain as well. A twenty-one-year study of senior citizens, aged seventy-five and older, at the Albert Einstein College of Medicine in New York City, found that dancing reduced the risk of dementia by an impressive 76 per cent.

At this point in time, you may not feel like going to clubs or other places where people are dancing just for fun. And in any case, a shortage of time and money may rule that option out. So why not invite yourself to dance in the privacy of your own home? You will reap exactly the same therapeutic benefits and maybe even more. One of the great advantages of secret solo dancing is that you can dance as wildly (and as badly!) as you like.

Better still, if you can create a safe enough space, try dancing with a blindfold on. It is an even more freeing and uplifting experience.

Steve, are normally good at responding assertively to people when they are annoying you, when you are stressed you often can't be bothered to 'fight' these minor battles. To avoid a build-up of irritation, try following the three simple steps below. You must put them into action as soon as you notice that you are beginning to feel impatient or annoyed. The longer you leave even mild anger to fester, the harder it is to deal with later.

1. Defuse

The 'Don't Get Too Boiling' strategy (see box, pp. 96–7) has been a favourite of mine for twenty years. These actions will send a message to your brain to switch off the anger response which has, among other auto-responses, caused your heart to start beating faster and your muscles to begin tensing up. Doing this will avoid a build-up of repressed feeling.

2. Review

Now that you are physically calm, you can engage your rational brain more easily to decide whether this is an issue that you need to deal with or not.

3. Confront or divert

Confront by assertively saying something like: 'I found myself getting irritated when you . . . ' (note – you are just communicating your feeling, not making an accusation). Then make a request: 'In future, would you please . . . '

Or, if you have chosen the divert option, find something engrossing to do which will help you forget the incident.

Flee into bliss with a float

Just prior to my fiftieth birthday I had been going through a particularly stressful few months, in the middle of which I lost a very great friend who had become my mother figure as well as my professional mentor.

I couldn't face a party celebration, so my husband took me away for a de-stressing and uplifting weekend instead. The condition was that every step of the weekend was under his control. I had to just be guided by him through each activity and would not have any idea of what I was going to do next. When I am stressed I have a strong tendency to become a control freak so, as you might imagine, this was a very major challenge for both of us!

Very wisely, for my first activity he chose to take me to a flotation centre. The result was that he was able to lead me around through treat after treat for the next forty-eight hours in a highly unusual state of consistent docility and serenity. By the Sunday afternoon, I was beginning to think I would never return to the real world again. But on Monday morning I woke up brimming with renewed energy and enthusiasm.

If you have ever taken a lilo on to a calm, warm sea or used float aids in a quiet swimming pool, you won't need convincing about its restorative effects. But now these have been scientifically proven to reduce the negative physiological effects of stress on the body.

A flotation centre contains small rooms with individual pools that are filled with water to which Dead Sea salts have been added. (These are renowned for increasing buoyancy.) The rooms are insulated from outside noise and also darkened. One research project in the United States revealed that when floating is done in such an environment, levels of cortisol (the stress hormone) are decreased by 21 per cent – an effect far greater than any you could achieve with similar rest on a lounger in a quiet dimly lit room.

Of course, you may not be lucky enough to have access to a flotation centre or a lilo on a warm sea right now. But you can simulate the 'floating-in-air' sensation using meditative techniques (see pp. 120–3). In my experience, these work best if you are lying in a warm bath that will help to relax your muscles; however, with a little practice, you can train yourself to achieve this 'floating' state anywhere – even sitting on a crowded, noisy train. You may not reach quite the same degree of relaxation as you would if you were lying in a flotation tank, but if you feel any kind of floating sensation you will know that you are reversing some of the negative physiological effects that stress has on your body.

Tap your troubles away with EFT

Lorraine, a sixty-three-year-old widow, had always dreamed of having a comfortable and reliable car. When she received an unexpected windfall in a bequest from an uncle, she decided to treat herself. One of her neighbours who had been a friend for twenty-five years had a business selling just the kind of car she had in mind. She knew his business had suffered badly during a recent international economic crisis, and thought that she would do him a favour and buy the car through him. A good deal was very quickly done.

Sadly, a few months later, it emerged that the car had been stolen. The police became involved and confiscated it immediately. Lorraine was devastated. Her friend maintained that all the registration papers had been in order and that he'd had no idea that the car was stolen. But nevertheless Lorraine had to take legal proceedings against him in order to recover her money. She had no money to buy another car, and being a widow of senior age she could not secure a loan from any bank.

For health and geographical reasons, Lorraine was dependent on a car to get around. When she was advised that she might not get any money back for several years she was thrown into a deeply anxious state. Friends could not get her out of her house or stop her from repeatedly blaming herself for having been too naive and impulsive, and also obsessively worrying about the court case and how she would manage without a car.

Luckily, one of Lorraine's daughter's friends was a counsellor who had just done a course in a relatively new therapy called the Emotional Freedom Technique (EFT). She offered to help and persuaded Lorraine to try it out. Much to everyone's surprise, it worked. Lorraine's emotional equilibrium quickly returned, and although she still had her practical problems to solve, she was able to return to her normal active life. And, very importantly, the risk of her slipping further down into a serious agoraphobic or depressed state was avoided.

What is the Emotional Freedom Technique?

The Emotional Freedom Technique (EFT) is one of the new 'power therapies', also known as 'energy psychology', and uses the ancient Chinese meridian energy system. It is based on the premise that negative emotions are the result of a disruption in the body's energy system. In principle, it is similar to acupuncture but doesn't use needles. Instead, well-established energy meridian points on your body are stimulated by tapping them with your fingertips.

The process of tapping these meridians clears blockages by sending pulses of energy to rebalance the body's energy system. Shifting this natural energy changes the way in which the brain processes information about a particular issue, and tapping, while tuned in to the issue in question, is like rewiring the brain's conditioned negative response.

Sandra Nathan, a counsellor at the Hale Clinic in London, specialises in EFT (see Resources, p. 265); she gave me a simple technique you can try on your own. It can be used on an everyday basis to prevent worries and self-destructive self-talk from taking a hold on you.

EFT self-help tap technique

Before starting, please note:

* that you do not need to tap hard; you are just trying to create a gentle vibration on the meridian

* you must tap seven times on average at each point

* you can use either hand and either side of the body, but you will find greater success when using both hands and tapping on both sides of the body at the same time, where possible.

Step 1

Think about the issue that's worrying you, then grade the intensity of the feeling (e.g. sadness, guilt, fear, etc.) that you are experiencing in relation to your specific issue on a simple scale of one to ten (where ten is the worst/highest level).

Step 2

Tap on your karate chop point (1. the side opposite the thumb of either hand – see below) while saying a positive reminder or affirmation such as: 'Even though I have this feeling of (...), I completely and utterly love and accept myself.'

Repeat this step three times.

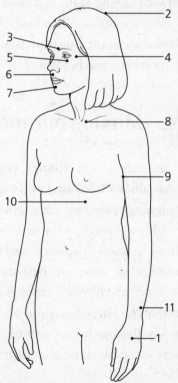

Step 3

Repeat your feeling statement and reminder phrase while tapping on each of the following points:

2. Top of your head

3. Beginning of your eyebrow (nearest your nose)

4. Side of your eye on the bone

5. Under your eye on the bone

6. Under your nose

7. Between your bottom lip and chin

8. Collar bone

9. Under your arm (about 7.5cm below armpit)

10. About 7.5cm below your nipple

11. Wrist point (on your arm, 2.5cm from the wrist joint)

Repeat this sequence.

Step 4

Take a deep breath, stretch, and check the intensity level of your feeling again. It should have reduced considerably.

If you want to chill out even further, you can continue to repeat the technique from step 2 until the intensity level of your feeling reaches zero.

 # Mimic your moans away

This may sound strange coming from someone who specialises in building self-esteem. But I do believe that laughing at yourself occasionally can be very useful.

This tip works in the same way as a little gentle teasing from a good friend or partner. I know that a bit of mimicking from my husband about my 'long face' or 'whiny' tone of voice can make me smile and snap myself out of the blues. You need to choose your moment sensitively though to humorously tease a loved one in this way – and the same is true for using this tip on yourself. It won't work if you are still very depressed, grieving or angry; when you are on the recovery road though and have just slipped off track a little, it can be very useful. So if you are aware (or have been made aware) that you are being a bit too gloomy for your own good, try this.

Stand in front of a full-length mirror and take a long, hard look at your body language. You may notice that your mouth is turning down slightly, that you are frowning or have let your shoulders droop. Next, exaggerate this body language and start to whine about your problems in an irritating, squeaky voice. Rev up your performance until you start smiling at the 'silly' image you see before you.

A variation of this technique can also be done with a friend or group of friends. You can have fun mimicking each other as we sometimes do in dramatherapy work-shops to lighten an overly heavy atmosphere. Or, if you happen to live near a hall of silly mirrors, you can get the same kind of boost by taking a trip there with a friend.

SECTION 4
Energise Your Body

Hi Gael – I'm all right, although working a lot. But I have upped my personal trainer sessions to twice a week! It has made a difference – to my mood, anyway!

Email from a former client going through a difficult time

O n receiving this message, I let out a massive sigh of relief; it reassured me that my client had turned a corner. She had rung me the previous month in a very upset state, having heard some disturbing news about her work situation. But this email told me that she was now doing what she needed to do in order to survive a tough period of high stress and insecurity.

Stress has a major debilitating effect on the body, so you need to take extra care with your health in tough times. You will need all the energy you can muster, even if your problem does not require much actual physical activity. While I am not a professional expert in this field, I do know from painful experience the effects of not taking good enough physical care of yourself during difficult times.

Most people under stress do the exact opposite of what my client did. They sideline their health maintenance routines, slacken off their exercise programmes and also often skip meals, eat unhealthy fast food and drink too much caffeine and alcohol. It is so important not to let this happen though. Doubling up on personal trainer time, as my client did, would probably be a mood-downer for me – and possibly for you too. Instead, I would increase my walks and stretching exercises in order to release my tension and get an extra supply of oxygen. But whatever health-care programme it is that works for you, be sure not to let it fall by the wayside. You need to take **more**, not less, care of your body during times of high stress.

This is why I've included this section with tips on basic care that have helped me and encouraged many others. So read on to find out what you can do to ensure your body gets the extra care it needs.

QUICK FIX: Eat for energy and health 80 per cent of the time

This is about achieving the right balance between sensible and sensual eating. Of course, most of the time you should eat food that keeps you physically healthy and will give you sustained energy. But we are all often motivated to eat foods that satisfy not just our nutritional needs, but also our sensual ones. And it's often during difficult times that the urge for 'comfort' eating kicks in.

This is why I suggest that you establish a percentage figure to help you. I recommend 80/20 as a guide for people with normal metabolism and no serious food disorders. This means that you take care to eat healthily and sensibly for the vast majority of the time (approximately 80 per cent). Then, for the remaining 20 per cent, you can allow yourself to eat for fun or speed with the occasional takeaway, restaurant or ready meal.

Note: extra care must be taken with non-sensible foods if you suffer with serious weight, diabetic or allergy issues.

> *Eating is not merely a material pleasure. Eating well gives a spectacular joy to life and contributes immensely to goodwill and happy companionship. It is of great importance to the morale.*
> **Elsa Schiaparelli, fashion designer**

Make fitness fun

Everyone knows how essential exercise is for physical health. But not enough attention is given to its power to improve emotional and mental wellbeing. You need it to oxygenate your brain into action and release tension so you can relax. The aerobic kind which makes you puff and sweat will also produce a surge of endorphins which induce feelings of wellbeing and pleasure.

During difficult times, normal fitness routines are often sidelined. Worry, anxiety and sadness all deplete your energy, so your usual trip to the gym or run round the park requires too much effort. In these times, you may have to change or adapt your exercise routine so that it feels easier and more enticing.

First, think about what stimulates enjoyment in you – we are all different in this respect. Then you can match one or more of these stimulators with some kind of uplifting exercise that you will enjoy. Here are just a few examples to give you the idea:

Stimulator	*Activity*
Adventure	Cycling or rambling with new friends to new places; mountaineering, kayaking
Competition	Competitive sports
Challenge	Stretching goals, such as marathons; classes for new skills; training for a bungee jump or difficult walking trek
Music	Dance; aqua-aerobics
Conversation	Rambling groups; ballroom dancing

Travel	Activity weekend breaks; cycling tours; river rowing
Animals	Walking dogs (you can borrow one!); horse-riding; walks around a zoo or animal park
Spiritual experiences	Yoga
Intellectual stimulation	Exercising at home while listening to radio discussions, quizzes or documentaries
Comedy	Rowing on a machine, while watching comic DVDs; comic relief sports events

Fitness – if it came in a bottle, everybody would have a great body.
Cher, singer and actress

 # Aim for quality sleep

Peter and Rebecca's son Charlie is a sergeant in the British army. At a time when the war in Afghanistan had started to re-escalate and was dominating the headlines in all the media, Charlie was posted to the front line. Understandably, neither Peter nor Rebecca was sleeping well. Both were becoming so exhausted that their insomnia was affecting their work and also their relationship. They were irritable with each other and spending much less time having fun together. Neither would consider taking sleeping tablets; they wanted to remain alert through the night in case they received a call from the army.

Peter and Rebecca were right to be concerned and seek advice. Research shows that sleep fragmentation and deprivation can have a negative effect on the brain for weeks. We have known for a long time how crucial sleep is for memory (see also p. 145), but new findings have shown that it also affects the ability to adjust to change and find new solutions.

QUICK FIX: Snack at a snail's pace

The little-and-often rule is good to remember in times of stress. Slow yourself down by stopping after every few mouthfuls to become aware of colours, shapes and textures on your plate, as well as the different sensations of taste. This will calm your troubled nerves, while at the same time making things easier for your digestive system. Chewing slowly gives the enzymes in your saliva longer to do their digestive work – breaking down some of the chemical bonds that connect the simple sugars that comprise starches. Also, there are some glands under your tongue whose secretions work on the digestion of fat – so the more snacking you do at a snail's pace, the more chance they have to do their job efficiently.

Great energising snacks to have in your pocket or on your desk are ones that need lots of chewing, such as dried vegetables and fruit and nuts.

I am sure that this isn't the news that you want to hear when you're going through tough times. The chances are that your normal sleep patterns have been severely disrupted and may well continue to be so for a long time. It's a fact of life for most people, but what can you do about it?

I advised Peter and Rebecca to stop counting the hours of sleep they were getting. Instead, I suggested that they try and ensure that the sleep they did have was the very best quality it could be. This gave them something positive to do, which is always a good way to divert the mind from worries.

If you are finding that you are getting less sleep than you need, take a look at the checklist below that I compiled for Peter and Rebecca. Try using it for a week or two – it really is vital that the hours of sleep that you do get are as restful and refreshing as they can be.

Conditions that aid quality sleep	*Have you . . .*
Tension-free muscles	❑ done your stretches and/or had a warm bath?
Dark room	❑ got an eyeshade by the bed; blackout lining behind curtains or blinds?
Low noise level	❑ got your earplugs, in case?
Carbohydrate snack	❑ eaten a nutritious small portion of cereal; rice or oat biscuit?
Calming drink	❑ tried a camomile infusion; milk?
Caffeine-free system	❑ made sure you haven't had coffee since lunchtime?
Low alcohol levels	❑ had one rather than two glasses of wine or beer?

Conditions that aid quality sleep	*Have you ...*
Comfortable temperature	❑ got a fan/heater on/extra blanket to hand?
Mind at ease	❑ written a to-do list and shelved it at least two hours ago?

And last, but not least, don't forget:

> *If you can't sleep, then get up and do something instead of lying there and worrying. It's the worry that gets you, not the loss of sleep.*
> **Dale Carnegie, personal development guru**

 ## Make sleep substitutes work for you

A flock of sheep that leisurely pass by
One after one; the sound of rain, and bees
Murmuring; the fall of rivers, winds and seas,
Smooth fields, white sheets of water, and pure sky –
I've thought of all by turns, and still I lie
Sleepless ...
William Wordsworth, poet

As I have suffered with periods of insomnia since early childhood, I have experimented with many sleep substitutes. Meditation is usually associated with achieving a spiritual 'boost', but it is also now a proven way of achieving deep relaxation. It puts your body into a low-powered state and enables it to perform many of its vital recovery functions.

Many meditation techniques require training and a substantial period of time and privacy, but here are two which are easy to learn, can be done in a short amount of time and are great as speedy re-energisers. They are particularly good for insomniacs or people who are chronically overtired. This is because there is less chance of falling asleep, as can often happen during longer meditations. They are also great for busy people because they can be done in public places. Perhaps my favourite way of using them, however, is during 'waiting time'; they stop people like me from using up energy getting anxious (or even angry) over how wasteful it is. Try them:

* during short train or plane journeys

* while standing in a very slow-moving or static queue

* when you are making a telephone call and know you will be on hold for a long while

* when you're waiting in the car, your office or home for latecomers.

The secret is to do these meditations regularly throughout the day. This will avoid a build-up of tension.

Three- to five-minute scenic meditation

1. Release the tension out of a few of your muscles by doing a few discreet stretches.

2. Close your eyes and recall in your mind a scene which conjures up for you a feeling of peace and wellbeing (a sunset on a favourite beach, a rose garden, a golf course or mountain path).

3. Visualise your scene in graphic detail. See its different colours and shapes. 'Listen' to its sounds and smell its scents.

4. Notice and enjoy the sensations of peace and wellbeing that you should now be feeling in your body. Allow yourself to relax even more in this sensation.

5. Take a couple of slow deep breaths and open your eyes.

Three- to five-minute mandala meditation

A mandala is a geometric design in which everything in the picture connects to a central point. There is an example of one below, but an image search on the Internet will bring up many other very beautiful and colourful ones. You could even draw or colour in your own. Keep it small enough that it fits easily into your handbag or pocket. You can then do this meditation almost anywhere.

Mandalas have been used for centuries all over the world to help induce a sense of inner peace. This meditation uses the hypnotic power of their design to quickly induce relaxation of your mind and body.

1. Adopt a relaxed posture – uncross any folded limbs and give your

A mandala for three- to five-minute meditation

shoulders a shrug or two. Put both feet on the ground in a comfortable position, slightly apart. Ensure that your back is straight and supported if you are sitting.

2. Take a few deep, slow breaths.

3. Focus your attention for 3–5 minutes on the central point of your mandala. If your attention begins to wander, just gently bring it back to the central point. As you relax, your mind will start to 'float' and your eyes will wander out to the sides of the design. When this happens gently refocus back again on the centre.

4. Bring yourself slowly back into the world by first squeezing your toes and fists, then taking a couple of slow breaths. Your mind should now feel clear and energetic. You may even have forgotten what you were worrying about. When you do remember, you may well have a new idea about how to solve the problem. This is because the mandala meditative process also stimulates the part of your brain that is home to your creative thinking 'muscles'. So this kind of meditation gives you two 'pay-offs' for the price of one!

SECTION 5
Boost Your
Brain Power

Difficult times can have a major negative effect on the brain. Your mind can feel 'fuzzy', so that you feel you just cannot 'think straight'; it can be filled with ideas or worries that whirl around relentlessly at an exhausting speed; or, of course, it can just 'go blank' at the very moment you need it most. A major trauma and prolonged stress can also have a detrimental effect on memory and the ability to concentrate.

A number of the tips in this section will help you to gain firmer control of your mind and keep it working in optimum power mode. This is so important when you are going through changes and often need your mind to feel sharper, so that you can think more quickly, as well as more laterally. There are also tips which will help you to 'feed' it literally, in nutritional terms, and also to stimulate its neural activity to enable you to think more positively and flexibly. And there are ideas which will help you to ensure that it has top-quality rest, even if your sleep is disturbed, as so often is the case at difficult moments in life.

Some of these tips will require a bit of study and concentration to learn, such as the Brain Gym exercises and the decision-making one (see pp. 128 and 149–53), but they can be so helpful that they are well worth the extra effort. Others, you'll be pleased to know, just give you full licence to take it easy and do what I know my teachers would have hated, namely more daydreaming and napping!

Take your brain to the gym

Live as if you were to die tomorrow. Learn as if you were to live for ever.
Mahatma Gandhi, leader of the Indian nationalist movement

Brain Gym (see Resources, p. 265) is a programme of physical exercises designed to stimulate brain activity that was originally developed by Dr Paul Dennison and his wife Gail in the 1970s and 1980s in the field of education in California. Despite many controversies about the scientific evidence for improving learning potential, Brain Gym is still widely used in educational establishments around the world and has many dedicated devotees.

I certainly do not claim to be an expert in this field, but there are a few exercises which I have personally used to good effect and have often suggested to clients. Below are a couple of appropriate ones for difficult times. If these work for you, you might want to find out more about the theories and practice of Brain Gym. Don't be put off by the scarcity of hard scientific evidence and cynics; good practitioners in their field are often ahead of the academic game, and there certainly doesn't seem to be anything to lose by doing some experimentation and research.

Cross-crawl

I like this exercise, not just because it is a great quick aerobic energiser, but also because it involves cross-lateral movements which help to stimulate the neural connections between the left and right brain hemispheres.

So it is a great one for us writers when we get stuck with that infamous 'writer's block'. Many educationalists also use it on a regular basis to improve spelling, writing, listening, reading and comprehension.

1. Standing or sitting, put your right hand across your body to your left knee as you raise it, then do the same thing for the left hand on the right knee, just as if you were marching.

2. Continue for at least 2 minutes.

Hook-ups

Here is another simple exercise that is perfect for use in difficult times. It works well for nerves before a challenging event, such as going for a job interview, seeing your bank manager or even going to a funeral. It will calm you down and help you to stay focused in the here and now.

1. Standing or sitting, cross your right leg over the left at the ankles.

2. Take your right wrist and cross it over the left wrist and link up the fingers so that the right wrist is on top (see Diagram 1, overleaf).

3. Bend your elbows out and gently turn your fingers in towards your body until they rest on the sternum (breast bone) in the centre of your chest (see Diagram 2, overleaf). Stay in this position.

4. Keep your ankles crossed and your wrists crossed, then breathe evenly in this position for a few minutes. You will be noticeably calmer after that time.

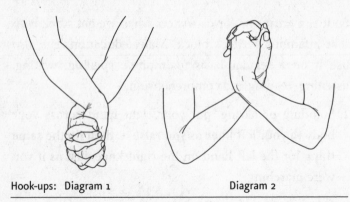

Hook-ups: Diagram 1   Diagram 2

Stimulate your spontaneity and creativity with an artistic challenge

The creative writing is going well. I am trying to work on a story about a boy whose grandfather gives him a family recipe that turns mean people purple. The plot is that he turns his teacher purple, not knowing that the recipe to reverse it has been lost! I do find it very difficult to read my work out in a group though (that old shyness comes back); it's very hard to share what I write. I am in two writing groups – one group I attend once a month and I really like the tutor and this group. We go out to the pub after the session and that's wonderful; everyone is very supportive and good fun.

Annette, fifty-one-year-old mother of a daughter with very serious health problems which frequently escalate into life-threatening crises

This is a recent email from Annette who originally came to see me because she needed training in confidence and assertiveness skills in order to be able to fight her daughter's battles with the health and social services. She had also started to have panic attacks and became fearful of going out, especially to places where she had to interact with people.

She learnt to manage her panic attacks and became one of the most competent people I ever met at managing to get the best out of the health and social services. But where she became stuck was when it came to looking for ways for her own needs to be fulfilled within her restricted lifestyle.

During our conversations it emerged that as a young girl Annette had a talent for creative writing. But her dream of being a writer had all her adult life been side-lined by her need to earn a living and bring up her family. We decided that a feasible activity for her would be to join a creative writing group. As the email indicates, this has proved to be very rewarding for her. The latest news is that her story did find an end and a publisher!

To stimulate her spontaneity and creativity, Annette has also now become involved with another group called the Red Hat Society (see Resources, p. 265). These are groups for women in middle age and beyond who meet all around the world. Their aim is to encourage social interaction, fun, silliness, creativity and friendship. Members must wear red hats and purple attire to all functions.

Difficult times often demand creative thinking. This is because past ways of doing and achieving may no longer be possible or appropriate. Ironically, when you are under severe stress your lateral thinking 'muscles' can virtually seize up. You need to be relaxed before new ideas can spring into your mind. How many great ideas arrive un-invited as you are out walking the dog or lying in the bath or half asleep in bed?

But rather than wait for this to happen, you can nudge this kind of thinking into action by doing anything that stimulates your spontaneity and creativity. Many artists use 'warm-ups' before they get down to serious work. In drama and dramatherapy sessions we play fun games that demand spontaneous responses. The artist will often just doodle or paint what comes into his or her head before starting back to serious work on a painting. Writers who have been hit by one of those famous 'blocks' usually stop for a break. Many of those I know also dabble in at least one other creative activity. So they will do something like improvising on the piano, dancing to jazz, 'playing' with paints, doodling or even going into the kitchen and concocting a new kind of meal out of whatever ingredients happen to be around.

So go ahead and be spontaneous. And if, as in the case of Annette, your artistic challenge is one that you have always wanted to try or were good at in your childhood, your morale boost will be even greater.

> *When I was forty, my husband left me unceremoniously. I felt he had just walked over a doormat. He suggested I got a secretarial job. Instead I bought a camera.*
> **Fay Godwin, photographer**

QUICK FIX: Debate with the enemy

> *I have never in my life learned anything from any man who agreed with me.*
> **Dudley Field Malone, civil rights lawyer**

Log on to a website which has opposite views to your own. For example, this could be the site of a newspaper that you wouldn't normally choose to read, or a group campaigning for a change in the law that you do not want or a fan club of music you don't like.

Open one of their chat pages and respond to some of the comments. But don't just have a rant; respond with a reasoned counter-argument. This should activate your brain cells!

 ## Flex your change muscles

> *A person needs at intervals to separate from family and companions and go to new places. One must go without familiars in order to be open to influences, to change.*
> **Katherine Butler Hathaway, poet and children's writer (she spent ten years of her life on her back, due to polio)**

Moving on from difficult times frequently demands that you make some kind of major change in your life. Major life changes could very well be:

* a change in your living arrangements through restricted finances

* a family break-up or loss

* a new medical condition or disability that needs to be accommodated

* needing to find a different kind of job

* new friends or a different partner

* a new psychological outlook or behaviour style.

Very few changes are easy rides, especially if they have been forced upon you, and it is human nature (even animal nature) to feel uncomfortable, frightened and often angry.

Where you have no choice in the matter and fighting back isn't an option, a common defence is to go into denial and say something like: 'Well, it might not happen anyway, and if it does I'll cross that bridge when I come to it.' But this kind of 'head-in-the-sand', fatalistic approach makes adjusting to change even more difficult.

To make the best of change, you have to embrace it confidently and positively. As someone whose whole life has been constantly peppered by change, I know that this does get easier (but still not easy) the more it happens. You become more accepting of emotional turmoil and are more wised-up on how to manage the feelings. You also learn to empower yourself by taking as much control as you can over the way the change happens. And, very importantly, you look after yourself better by taking lots of support while you are making the adjustment.

You'll cope better still with the bigger and more frightening changes if you keep your 'change muscles' well exercised. A little practice at making some small adjustments in your life, your way of doing things or your outlook can help you to feel much more at ease when it comes to weathering the bigger transitions.

Below are some examples of the practical 'homework' exercises that I suggest to clients who know they have to take a big leap forward into some kind of new life or lifestyle. Keeping some notes on how you felt before, during and after the change is very useful. Not only do you find out what helps and what doesn't, you also become more aware of what to expect in terms of your emotional reaction.

Suggestions for gently flexing your change muscles

* Read a bestselling book that you wouldn't normally be attracted to.

* Visit somewhere you have never been to and, if possible, use a different method of transport to make the journey.

* Eat out at a restaurant or café that serves a kind of food you have never tried before.

* Go to a religious service or ritual occasion of a faith you know very little about.

* Participate in a festival from another culture.

* Try a sport that you have never tried; those that involve others work best. Most clubs or associations will be only too willing to let you try your hand.

* Do an activity with people from a different age group.

* Make an extravagant purchase if you are normally frugal (don't overstrain the budget though).

* Live on next to nothing for a week if you have a relatively comfortable income.

* Go to the cinema on your own (unless you already do so).

* Change your hairstyle or colour.

* Exchange some household tasks with other members of the family.

Finally, as you go through your changes, notice how you as a person are subtly adjusting and developing. For me, that is the most exciting part of moving on and I am still constantly surprised by the way change can change me and others. If you manage your transitions well, the change in you is sure to be a positive one that will enrich your life.

> *The most important thing to remember is this: to be ready at any moment to give up what you are for what you might become.*
> **W. E. B. du Bois, civil rights activist**

 # Practise positive thinking

It's no news nowadays that positive thinking is good for you. Mountains of research have proved that it benefits your health, and makes successful outcomes more likely in work, personal relationships and sporting life. It has also proved (surprise, surprise!) that people with an optimistic outlook are more resilient to setbacks and tough experiences.

For some lucky people, thinking positively is an auto-response that their brain produces when faced with any challenge. They will always see that silver lining around the grey cloud and count on the sun shining in their favour once again.

But there are many people who automatically react in quite the opposite way. They only see the emptiness in the half-filled glass. In setback situations, they focus first and foremost on the potential problems and are blind to any opportunities.

Why is there such a marked difference? Some people are undoubtedly blessed by their genes and have naturally sunny dispositions. Others appear to emerge from the womb destined to become cry babies forever after. But subsequent life experience can also play a significant part.

We know now that, especially at an early age, the way we are nurtured and the role modelling to which we are exposed affects the emotional neural wiring. So those who immediately focus on the emptiness in the half-glass have commonly had negative-thinking parents or teachers or repeatedly had disappointing or unhappy experiences in childhood. As a result, their brains needed to develop the auto-responses of anticipating the problems and fearing the worst as necessary survival strategies in preparation for fighting, fleeing or simply 'shutting down'.

Similarly, people who have been exposed to repeated or highly dramatic emotional trauma during their adult lives can also be hard-wired with these kinds of negative-thinking responses. Common examples would be soldiers returning from violent war zones or survivors of a major disaster in which many were killed and maimed. Even people who were previously naturally optimistic can emerge from these dreadful experiences with a complete personality change.

If your default thought mode tends to be negative, you should first reflect on what may be at the root of your problem. If you believe that it is caused just by bad luck of the draw from Mother Nature, then the simple positive-thinking strategy below should be sufficient to help you. If, however, your dark auto-outlook has been fed by some seriously negative life experiences, you may need to do some emotional healing before you can reprogramme yourself to think positively most of the time. To do this you could try healing yourself using my book *The Emotional Healing Strategy* (see Resources, p. 265) as a guide or, of course, you could seek professional help from a counsellor or therapist. In the meantime, try this technique too. It should certainly start to help you, especially in everyday challenging situations.

The GEE strategy

This is a great technique for breaking out of a negative-thinking rut. When you (or anyone else) notices that you are thinking pessimistically, ask yourself the following three simple questions. Then try to rephrase your thoughts from a positive viewpoint.

1. Am I **G**eneralising from one or a few specific experiences?

   Original thought: 'Everyone is too busy to help you nowadays.'

   Rephrased thought: 'Most people are willing to make time; Jane is an exception.'

2. Am I **E**xaggerating current problems, potential hazards or difficulties?

   Original thought: 'This new restriction is going to cause chaos at the airport; I can just see us spending the night there.'

   Rephrased thought: 'This new restriction is going to mean longer queues until everyone gets used to it, so we must be prepared for some delays for the next month or so.'

3. Am I **E**xcluding any positive aspects or potential?

   Original thought: 'That woman's incapable of caring – she just thinks of number one full stop. I'm sure all she was concerned about was getting off the phone so she could get home on time. There's no point in ringing her again.'

   Rephrased thought: 'Her response when I rang yesterday was certainly a bit abrupt. Let's hope I just caught her at a bad time . . . perhaps if I try ringing her again in the morning and tell her that I didn't get a chance to explain the full story, she'll hear me out and have some suggestions.'

Free your mind from auto-thoughts

Change your thoughts and you change your world.
Norman Vincent Peale, positive thinking guru and writer

Carl, a professional photographer in his early fifties, was driving home from a new friend's house in the country one evening. In a momentary lapse of concentration, he took a right turn instead of a left one and found himself facing oncoming traffic on a dual carriageway. The result was a crash in which a woman was killed.

Carl was given a fifteen-month prison sentence. He had not drunk any alcohol and had a clean twenty-three-year driving record. He had never been in any kind of trouble with the law before. A caring, sensitive and highly responsible man, he had never in his wildest nightmares thought that he would spend time in prison. He was terrified.

In order to help him cope with the devastating thoughts and feelings about what he had accidentally done and its consequences, Carl is constantly looking for ways to extract something positive out of his prison experience. This extract from one of his letters to me is an example:

> Deprived of society's usual distractions, I have nowhere to hide in the short term, in terms of facing my fears and some of my habitual thought patterns

that I took for granted as being part of myself and my life. I have stepped out of the pattern of being continually lost in thought and any emotion that would trigger. I have learnt to stand back and witness my own thoughts as they are happening. This has given me a choice. I can choose to pay attention to the thought or let it pass. Before, I would give all thoughts equal weight and believe I would have to get to the bottom of all of them and their corresponding emotion – in effect, always to 'solve' problems.

It is hard to describe, but I have become able to witness my thoughts as a presence behind them, rather than being swept along by them without any awareness or wider choice. This is my freedom.

I believe Carl's strategy is one that can be used in many other difficult situations as well. When you go through hard times, it is easy to be at the mercy of thoughts that enter your mind without your conscious consent; they can make you feel fearful, guilty, pessimistic, regretful or even powerless, when the reality is that you are confident and capable enough to deal positively with your problem.

If this happens to you, remember Carl's trick of imagining himself as an observer of his thoughts, with the freedom to be able to choose which ones you will pursue and which you will let go.

You might also like to try a variation, which is to give your thoughts a pictorial representation. One of the most popular choices is to imagine the thoughts encircled by clouds. You can then decide to see them as heavy, grey ones or light, wispy ones set against a blue sky or the warm glow of a beautiful sunrise. Then it is up to you whether you choose to dwell on your thoughts or just let them drift slowly – or quickly – by.

 # Use 'scrap' time to stretch your mental muscles

I tried to think of it as a journey of self-exploration.
Terry Waite, British hostage held in Beirut

I hope none of you reading this have had such a testing challenge as Terry Waite's, but many other ongoing problem situations can require that you 'sit it out' for a period of time:

* After a bereavement, it can take many months until the will is finally sorted.

* An illness may require that you 'do nothing' for a time, while tests are done or various treatments are tried; or you may need an extended period of convalescence.

* In a credit crisis, you are usually advised to 'sit tight' until the financial winds blow more favourably.

* After a separation or a divorce it can take a long time for financial and access matters to be sorted.

* Parents of difficult teenagers are told to be patient and just 'be there' until they 'grow out of it', so they put their own plans on hold.

* After a redundancy, there may be long periods of waiting for the right job to come up and not being able to make many plans so that you can be ready and available in case you are called for an interview.

* If you are involved in a legal process, you may not be given much notice of when your presence will be quickly required.

* If you are living in a war zone you may not be able to move on in the way you would like to until peace returns.

These are times when a sense of personal powerlessness can creep in. There is then a real risk of slipping into depression or going into a kind of apathetic or even a zombie-style mental state. This is especially so if the crisis has been a big one and has required a great deal of 'fire-fighting' action. One way of ensuring that you remain positive and your mind stays sharp is to view this period as a great opportunity for personal learning and development.

Below are some examples of what has helped others to do this. Bear in mind that you will reap the most benefit if you choose to do something that you are not already good at and that also has some pleasurable motivating appeal for you.

Ways to use scrap time to stretch your brain's mental agility

* Buy or borrow a Brain Trainer (a hand-held electronic 'toy' designed to stimulate your thinking and memory

powers through word and number 'games', usually created in conjunction with neuroscientists). My husband's short-term memory improved demonstrably after my daughter gave him one of these for Christmas.

* Become a puzzle freak. All manner of puzzles can be picked up very cheaply in second-hand or charity shops. Or just ask your neighbours if they have any they are not using. These could be a jigsaw, crossword, Sudoku, Rubik cube, word search or anything else that you don't usually do.

* Go to a pub, church or company quiz night or, better still, offer to join the team!

* Learn a new language and give yourself real-life opportunities to practise.

* Invent stories for your children instead of just reading to them.

* Read self-help books . . . and actually do what they recommend!

* Do a short cookery course and improvise with recipes.

* Do an Open University short course which requires you to think for yourself and not just acquire information.

* Learn a new computer programme or how to use a facility you need, but thought you couldn't master. (With my next piece of scrap time I will learn how to create an Excel spreadsheet!)

* Learn a skill that will be useful at home: how to put up shelves, prune roses, regrout tiles and mend a leak are

just a few on my pending list. Use your friends and neighbours as teachers and offer to do something for them in return.

QUICK FIX: Get napping

Neuroscientists have recently found that a nap can, in a similar way to daydreaming, boost the brain's relational memory function. While you are dozing away, your brain is doing some very important filing work. It creates conceptual connections between masses of independent details, enabling you to retrieve memories much more quickly and apply the learning from them more widely.

Another piece of research published in 2008 compared the positive effects of napping on the memory to a more widely used brain energiser – caffeine. Guess which came out the winner?

A nap can take place almost anywhere. Some people can do it standing up, waiting in a queue, but most find that they need to take theirs dozing in a chair or lying on a flat surface. Ten to fifteen minutes is usually the optimum time for a nap or siesta. Research has shown that after 30 minutes or longer you are likely to fall into a deeper sleep which will leave you feeling groggy, rather than refreshed.

Bore your brain into daydream mode

Every time you let yourself slip into a daydream, your brain starts to work in an important way on your behalf. Neuroscience has revealed that it goes into a mode that is now thought to be its 'default network', and while in this state, certain interconnected areas are activated. This particular kind of activity makes new connections between seemingly unrelated ideas and information. As a result, new perceptions and ideas generate creative activity.

I have known about the creativity-boosting potential of daydreaming for many years. However, I have always thought that this very useful mental state is best induced through deep relaxation, which usually entails setting aside a sizeable chunk of time in order to unwind – and even more time if you happen to be stressed out by the kind of problems that tough times can bring.

So I was very interested to learn that the research now indicates that this default network is most often activated when we are engaged in performing routine tasks that require very little conscious attention or when we are listening to something that we find rather boring. If your everyday life is anything like mine then you will no doubt be able to think of many examples of such tasks:

* Clearing up after a meal

* Standing in a queue at the supermarket, station or airport

* Travelling on public transport when it is too noisy and busy to be able to use the time for reading or listening to music

* Going to a boring lecture or presentation which is delivered with a deadly drone

* Attending a routine meeting, just to show your face

* Watching a film at the cinema that you find boring but which your companion is glued to

* Sweeping away leaves or snow in the garden

* Waiting in a doctor's surgery

* Ironing

So you can now let your mind have a guilt-free wander when you find yourself in one of these situations. Indeed, Arthur Fry, inventor of the sticky yellow Post-it notes, is said to have come up with his very clever idea while daydreaming through a tedious sermon.

There is just one catch though: you must retain some conscious control over your daydreaming. In order for this state to be productive, you need to be aware enough of what you are doing to be able to notice a bright idea. This is why daydreaming while still engaged in some kind of task – even if that is only listening with half an ear – is better than floating off into a less conscious state.

If you happen to be the kind of person who is never bored and who is lucky enough to have someone else to do all your mindless chores for you, read the previous tip on napping!

Eat complex foods and ban brain foggers

Avoid the simple carbohydrates which may give you instant cheer and energy, but will soon cloud your mind and depress your mood. You may well already know what they are, but here's a reminder of the worst offenders:

✗ Cakes

✗ Sweets

✗ Biscuits

✗ Soft drinks

Ensure your alertness by eating instead complex meals containing a balance of protein and vegetables or fruit and drinking lots of water or green tea. Also, keep a supply of alternative snacks prepared and at the ready. Fill a shelf of your fridge with the types of food that neuroscience research has shown to energise the thinking brain (you could also take a selection around with you in a small insulated box). Here are some suggestions:

✔ Chunks of cooked lean chicken or turkey

✔ Chunks of cooked salmon, sardines, tuna or mackerel

✔ Shrimps or prawns

✔ Cubes of marinated organic tofu

✔ Hummus with carrot, pepper and raw broccoli sticks

✔ Walnuts and Brazil nuts with sunflower seeds

✔ Oatcakes or brown rice cakes

✔ Brown rice or pasta

✔ Low-fat cottage cheese with avocado slices dipped in lemon juice

✔ Lentil, aubergine and pepper salad with miso dressing

✔ Chickpea and broccoli and mushroom salad or stir-fry

✔ Spinach, asparagus and lettuce salad

✔ Blueberries/raspberries/orange segments/ blackberries/kiwi fruit

✔ Low-fat yoghurt to mix with any of the above fresh fruits

Deal decisively with dithering

Nothing is more difficult, or therefore more precious than the ability to decide.
Napoleon Bonaparte, French military leader and emperor

Difficult times often confront us with seriously difficult decisions such as:

＊ Where do I live now?

＊ How do I earn my living now?

＊ Should I get a divorce or not?

＊ Should I try for the same kind of job or train for something different?

✳ Should I have this risky operation or not?

✳ Should I tell the police or not?

One of the knock-on effects of these pending dilemmas is that everyday choices like, 'Tea or coffee?' or, 'What should I wear?' begin to feel stressful. It's as though your brain's decision-making powers have just frozen up.

If this has started to happen to you, I hope it helps to know that it's normal and understandable. First of all, give yourself a break from making the minor decisions and delegate these whenever you can. Reserve your energy for the more important ones.

Next, for one important decision that you are concerned about, follow the ten-step strategy below. Doing this will help you because it stimulates the thinking centres in your brain and eases you out of the predominating emotional state which is stopping you from thinking clearly.

Ten steps to making a good decision

1. Set a date/time for your decision day or hour.

2. Gather information – consult research; write down facts; consult others with information, experience and opinions to share.

3. Make a 'Decision Factors List', highlighting the key elements that have a bearing on your choice. I've given an example on p. 151), but it is important to select factors that are relevant to your particular decision. The number of categories you have will depend on the complexity of the decision.

In the example that follows, the person has highlighted six key aspects with regard to choosing a career and put them in priority order, where six is the most important.

Decision factor	*Priority order*
❏ Minimises financial pressure	4
❏ Easier to implement	1
❏ Involves a low level of risk	3
❏ Motivational for me	6
❏ Minimal disruption for my family	5
❏ Morally OK for me	2

4. Next, draw a grid like **Grid A** on p. 152, listing your choices on the left-hand column, with the decision factors in the columns on the right. Rate your decision factors on a scale of one to three, where one is the least likelihood of achieving them.

5. Now give yourself a break – try to do something absorbing that takes your mind off the subject and, preferably, relaxes you. If possible, sleep on it for one night.

6. Review what you have written and, if necessary, make changes to your scores. Then, once you are happy with the scores, multiply all your ratings of three by the rank order number you allocated in your original decision-factor list. Then add all the scores for each choice together. So the new grid would look like **Grid B** on p. 152.

7. Your total column should reveal the 'winner' – i.e. the one with the highest mark. If it's a 'draw', repeat the exercise with those factors that scored two and this will provide a result. However, bear in mind in such

Decision grids

Grid A

Choices	Decision factors					
	Minimises financial pressure	Easier to implement	Low risk	Motivational for me	Minimal disruption for family	Morally OK for me
A: Stay in boring job – poor prospects/salary	2	3	2	1	3	1
B: Pursue new job offer – better prospects/salary (involves moving)	3	2	3	3	2	3
C: Leave job to become self-employed	1	1	1	2	1	2

Grid B

Choices	Decision factors						Total
	Minimises financial pressure	Easier to implement	Low risk	Motivational for me	Minimal disruption for family	Morally OK for me	
A: Stay in boring job – poor prospects/salary	2	3 x 1 = 3	2	1	3 x 5 = 15	1	18
B: Pursue new job offer – better prospects/salary (involves moving)	3 x 4 = 12	2	3 x 3 = 9	3 x 6 = 18	2	3 x 2 = 6	45
C: Leave job to become self-employed	1	1	1	2	1	2	0

circumstances that there may be very little to choose between the options, so you may need to give further serious thought to the pros and cons related, I would suggest, to the most important decision factors.

8. Write down your final decision – most people have more commitment to written resolutions.

9. Share it with certain people; these should be people who can commit to asking you at a certain time later whether you implemented your decision.

10. Act as quickly as you can to implement your decision. At the very least, take one action almost immediately that will kick off the process. This will help seal your commitment and give you a great morale boost at the same time.

> *The worst thing you can do is to wait until a decision is forced on you – or made for you.*
> **John S. Hammond, author and expert in decision-making and former professor of the Harvard Business School**

SECTION 6
Mobilise Your Motivation

Whatever has caused your current situation may well also have destroyed part (or all) of any life dream that drove you forward. You may suddenly find that the goals that kept you going no longer have so much meaning for you. The prospects of money, love or even happiness often lose some, if not all, of their emotional pull, and it is quite easy to slip into a state of apathy or cynicism about the future.

Of course, the irony is that to move on successfully after a setback, you need more motivation than you had before, not less. One of the problems people find is that their opportunities are more restricted and that they have to look and 'fight' harder than they may have anticipated. If, for example, you have been made redundant, it is likely that there will be more competition for fewer suitable jobs. Or, if you have been through a divorce, you may find that your 'rivals' are younger or that they have fewer fixed commitments than you do. And should you have a health problem that has left you with a disability, you may find it a lot harder to lead a 'normal' kind of life than you'd expected, in spite of all the help and aids you were promised while still in hospital. This is why you need – and deserve – powerful doses of quality inspiration to kickstart you into action.

The tips in this section will encourage you to look forward, rather than back, and to avoid those people who make a habit of highlighting problems and predicting doom and gloom. There are ideas here to help you keep your 'dream' goals alive, so they can continually drip-feed you with inspiration. You will also be encouraged to raise your spirits with the thrill of growing plants, clearing the clutter from your environment and stimulating your sense of humour and fun.

> *You may encounter many defeats, but you must not be defeated. In fact, it may be necessary to encounter the defeats, so you can know who you are, what you can rise from, how you can still come out of it.*
> **Maya Angelou, author, actress and human rights activst**

QUICK FIX: Be wary of nostalgia

> *Nostalgia is a file that removes the rough edges from the good old days.*
> **Doug Larson, writer**

Recent research has revealed that the brain is very selective about the memories it stores. For example, it favours the best and worst of times, and also has something of an obsession with endings. So if an outcome was *eventually* good (such as holding your newborn in your arms), that is the memory that will be clear and bright. Your memory of the long, drawn-out labour, the sweat and tears will be recorded minimally in comparison.

Of course, indulging in nostalgia can sometimes make you feel good, but in difficult times, the danger is that it will leave you with feelings of regret that today and tomorrow can't be as good.

Remember also that consistent, lasting happiness is not necessarily punctuated with ecstatic, memorable moments, which means that we are less likely to recall it.

So whenever you find yourself regretting that you can't turn the clock back, remind yourself that your brain might have got it wrong, and return your focus to doing all you can to make your present and future as rewarding as they can be.

Get growing something

At forty-five, Adrian was diagnosed with a motor neurone disease and it appeared to be progressing quite rapidly. Not only would it affect his capacity to work as an electrical engineer, it also threatened his ability to enjoy his hobby – archery. From an early age Adrian had shown a talent for archery, had now become captain of his regional team and had started coaching a new team of wheelchair archers. Most of his social life revolved around this sport.

Although Adrian was determined to be positive in the face of his daunting diagnosis, he was inwardly very fearful of the restrictions that this invasive disease would put on his life.

One day, over lunch at work, his wife, Fay, was sharing her concerns about him with a group of colleagues. They were a group of very caring and practical women and were quick to come up with loads of alternative interests and hobbies. But one idea shone out as having the most possible appeal to Adrian. One woman had been involved in a fund-raising event for an organisation called Thrive (see Resources, p. 266), which she knew had been a great help to a friend who had developed multiple sclerosis. She explained that this small national charity used gardening to change the lives of disabled people.

Fay knew that Adrian might consider this as an option because only a month previously, when they were sitting in their untidy jungle of a garden, Adrian had said that it was a pity that in their busy lives the gardening always fell to the bottom of their priority lists.

Adrian did decide to contact Thrive. The local organiser happened to live quite near by, so he popped round to explain their work further. Needless to say, he took a great interest in Adrian's wheelchair archery project and the two men instantly became friends. One year on, with the help of a team from Thrive, Adrian's garden is now an oasis of flowering tranquillity and two of Thrive's wheelchair-bound members are learning archery. Adrian plans to stay involved with the archery club when his illness progresses, if only in an advisory capacity, but he now knows that he has another hobby that will be just as challenging and absorbing which he can move on to.

> *To be happy for an hour, get drunk; to be happy for a year, fall in love; to be happy for life, take up gardening.*
> **Chinese proverb**

Thrive has completed a number of research studies which show that gardening can help people going through all sorts of difficult periods in their lives. Janet Caruso, who works for the organisation, explains: 'Gardening can help you get back on top of things and restore the balance when it feels like your life is veering out of control. It helps you to feel happier, more confident and healthier.' She gave the following reasons why it can be such a great morale booster and positive diversion for anyone who may be at a low time in their life:

* It is great physical exercise.

* You can work at your own pace and in small steps.

* You can learn new skills which might be useful in other areas of your life.

* It can provide a great opportunity to meet people.

* It can offer an opportunity for self-expression and a chance to explore your creativity.

* Nurturing growing things can literally give you a reason to get out of bed in the morning and the satisfaction of knowing that you have made it happen.

* If you are finding everyday life hard to cope with, gardening outside could even help you to take a first step out of the house.

Like Adrian and Fay, I have very little time in my life for gardening. But I do know that just dead-heading a few roses or pulling the dead leaves off my poor houseplants works as a calming and satisfying diversion. So even if you only have time and space to grow a box of cress or plant a pot of bulbs, try this nurturing therapy.

 # Uncover the possibilities for progress

Discontent is the first necessity of progress.
Thomas A. Edison, scientist and inventor

The great American inventor Thomas Edison's own life story is a great example of this piece of wisdom in action. It also demonstrates how you can learn its lesson the hard way by living through tough times.

Thomas, the last of seven children, experienced his first serious period of discontent in early infancy. He didn't learn to talk until he was four years old which, for a child with such an enquiring and demanding mind, must have been torture. Thomas was later asked to leave his school because the teachers were so aggravated by his behaviour and lack of progress; his mind continually wandered from the task he was given. With the knowledge we now have about learning problems, we can guess that he had some kind of attention deficit disorder. We could also make a good guess that his problems had a lot to do with being a gifted child in a school environment which could not hope to satisfy his quick-thinking and creative mind.

As if the set-up of Thomas's brain didn't already bring him more than his fair share of discontent, he also suffered from a hearing disability. This appears to have started in childhood and become progressively worse in adulthood. No doubt his frustrations with this particular difficulty had some bearing on his interest in developing one of his later inventions – the phonograph.

In his early teen years, on his own initiative, he started to sell sweets and newspapers on trains as a way of supplementing his income. Again, something positive was to emerge from this enforced need to make money – he would become one of the greatest entrepreneurial businessmen of his era.

However, it was his developed character trait of positive persistence in the face of seemingly impossible odds that helped him most to become a man who is commonly considered to be the father of the electrical and technological revolution that would change the world so dramatically. When he first encountered the earliest light bulb, fifty years of effort had already been spent on trying to make this remarkable invention become commercially viable.

So when you find yourself struggling to believe that anything positive can emerge from the frustration of challenge after challenge, remind yourself of Edison's story and another of his famous quotes:

> *I have not failed. I've just found ten thousand ways that won't work.*
> **Thomas Edison, scientist and inventor**

QUICK FIX: Shun the grumpy but not the occasional grumble

A good grumble to a friend or acquaintance is a great way to express your feelings. But make sure that it is to the kind of friend who is essentially a positive person and one who will comfort you. Avoid full-time moaners who are guaranteed to make you feel even worse because they are compelled to top your story with a stream of even greater problems of their own.

Cure bouts of despair with humour

However hard you may try to keep thinking positively, bouts of despair are likely to kick in from time to time.

Sometimes, if you catch them early, humour can help to snap you out of them. Laughter releases tension, and laughing together with a group of people can bring you closer so that you become more mutually supportive.

In the weeks following my nineteen-year-old daughter's death, I was frequently at the point of total despair. One afternoon, I was in such a state when a group of Laura's close friends and her boyfriend came round to see me. Like my daughter, they too were in their late teens. None of them had ever had to face a loss and shock such as this. Not only had they lost someone who they loved and had been, in their words, 'the leading light' of their group, they also had to face the fragility of life, even for people of their young age. Because they were in this emotionally turbulent state and still very young, they acted very spontaneously, with very little concern about what was the wrong or right way to behave in this situation. They cried and hugged me, as well as each other, but then they sat down and began recalling lots of fun times with Laura and, in particular, funny things she had done and said. We found ourselves roaring with laughter as each person (including me) shared their humorous anecdotes.

If someone had told me before this happened that I might take part in such a 'session' so soon after the death of one of my daughters, I would have forcibly assured them that this would not be possible. I had to live through this experience to believe it could happen and also to accept that, even in this stage of raw grief, laughter about a deceased loved one has the power to heal and positively bond people together.

Psychologists specialising in research into this subject report that joking appears to be a genuine psychological need in the face of bad situations, and is common even in major disasters and horrific war situations. Prisoners of war in Vietnam who were in solitary confinement found they could tap out jokes to each other through their walls. Hostages like Brian Keenan and John McCarthy have both said that the sense of humour that they shared helped them to bond together in spite of differences in their backgrounds and personalities. Psychologists have suggested that as well as being a stress reliever, humour can help because it gives you a sense of power.

If your problems are in any way due to illness or infirmity, laughter is especially important, as it stimulates the flow of oxygen around your body. Laughing regularly produces more endorphins and encephalin, which lift your mood and suppress pain. Laughter also produces a protein called immunoglobin which is known to kill germs and promote the white blood cells which fight off infection. The more intense and regular the laugh, the more oxygen flows around your body and the more toxic carbon dioxide is released.

So although you may not feel like doing so, make a special effort to ensure that you experience more of the things which are likely to trip you into a humorous mood such as:

* watching comedies

* having fun nights out with humorous friends (laughter is infectious)

* dipping into books of cartoons or humorous quotations.

The more one suffers, the more, I believe, one has a sense of the comic. It is only by the deepest suffering that one acquires the authority in the art of the comic.

Søren Aabye Kierkegaard, philosopher

Make a drama out of your dream

Thirty-five-year-old Teresa was someone who had apparently drifted haphazardly into a number of different careers. Three months before I saw her she had been told that it was possible that there would be a departmental restructure in the near future. Having heard this euphemism before, she knew that this was a strong hint that her job was at risk. Her boss kindly suggested that when Teresa considered her next job move, she should ensure she takes some time out first to help her make a well-thought-through career decision rather than a desperate jump into the first option that came available.

Teresa was persuaded by a friend to join her on one of my 'Moving On' courses in Spain. She started by saying that she didn't want to waste our time as she didn't think there was much hope of her changing: 'I'm a starter and not a finisher,' she said. 'I get all these ideas and have all these dreams about what I could do, but I never follow through on my plans.'

We used psychodrama to explore the root cause of her motivational problem which lay mostly in her busy, harassed parents' lack of interest in her development and success. Then the group helped her to bring her dream career to life.

Since travelling around the world in her early twenties, Teresa had dreamed about having her own specialist travel agency. So we played out various highly positive scenarios with Teresa in the star role as owner of an eco-tourism agency, offering holidays in Africa. Then, later that evening, the group threw her a celebration party. They pretended she had won a Business Woman of the Year award. They toasted her with sparkling wine and made a giant celebration poster. One person took the role of playing the High Commissioner of Uganda and presented her with a colourful certificate that had been painted by another participant.

On her return home, Teresa pinned her certificate up in her bedroom, together with photos of the celebratory event the group had organised. This helped her recall and relive the wonderful fun she'd had with them enacting her dream. Several group members kept in contact with her, enquiring as to how her career dream plans were developing.

Teresa is now working for a travel company operating safaris in Africa with a view to learning the trade. She is having a wonderful time and appears to have an aptitude for the business. She believes that the dramatisation of her dream totally changed both her and her life.

Psychodrama is just one way that can help you to make a drama out of your dream. But it is certainly not the only way. You could invite your friends over for a 'dream drama party', which would work just as well as a motivator.

Creative visualisation

You can also use creative visualisation to bring your dream to life by creating a motivating drama in your head. Here are six simple steps to help you do this:

1. Find as quiet a place as possible. Ideally, this would be in a private, sound-proofed room where you could lie down and close your eyes. But if this is not available, just stay standing or sitting where you are in a relaxed posture. This would mean uncrossing any crossed limbs, putting both feet on the ground and ensuring that your body feels balanced and supported in the best way it can be.

2. Take two or three deep slow breaths while focusing your mind on your breath going in and out of your body. The out-breath should take a little longer than the in-breath, and it is helpful to stay in 'pause position' for a few seconds between the in- and out-breaths. This breathing technique should take you into quite a deeply relaxed state, but one in which you are still aware and conscious.

3. Use your imagination to play a mental movie in your mind of your dream coming true. Notice all the details in your movie such as:

   * the colours, sounds and shapes

   * the people and objects around

   * yourself – how do you look? How do you sound? And, very importantly, try and sense how you are feeling and reacting in this scene.

4. Imagine that you can turn up the definition of the movie. Increase the volume and brightness and the sensations and relax even more, giving yourself up to the experience without thinking or judging it. Just enjoy it.

5. Bring yourself back into the world by taking a couple of deep breaths and having a stretch.

6. Repeat this visualisation two or three times over the coming week to ensure that the 'false memory' of your dream being realised is firmly planted in your subconscious mind.

Write a song

Another idea might be to write a song about the realisation of your dream and sing it regularly to yourself. This worked particularly well for one of my clients, especially as her dream was to become a professional songwriter! She has now reduced her job to a three-day week and writes and performs on the other two days.

These kinds of creative techniques will increase your motivation because they 'trick' your mind into thinking that achieving your dream is much more of a real possibility because it has 'happened' before. Sports stars have been using them for years. Even if you are not looking for a radical change of career or lifestyle at the moment, this tip could still give you some other benefits: they are fun and confidence-building too.

Clear the clutter

Whose home couldn't do with at least some clutter clearance?

We moved house nearly three years ago to much smaller accommodation. We must have halved our possessions at that time, but we still clung on to a lot and filled a large storeroom with it. To this day, we haven't even discussed entering this room. And, I am now finding it hard to even recall what is in there that we thought was too important to lose!

Clearing your home of accumulated clutter is a simple energising task that never fails to leave you with a self-satisfied smile. It is also one that inevitably stimulates envy and elicits admiring comments from friends and neighbours. Because it has such self-esteem-boosting and motivational powers, I often suggest it as therapeutic 'homework' for clients. It is particularly good as a constructive interim task when you are feeling depowered by the 'big' difficulties or when you have to wait for something to be resolved or clarified before you can move on. It also works well as a healing 'closure' ritual when you want to say 'goodbye' to a relationship, job or home.

Here are a few tips to help you clear some clutter:

* Take three rubbish bags or boxes and label them: 'Charity', 'Recycling' and 'Rubbish'.

* Set a date and time for completing your task. This could be the same day or it could be a week or month later so that you complete the task over some weeks. But

whatever the time frame you choose, start with one major sorting session as soon as you can.

* Try to stay guided by your first impulse to let go of something. It is almost always right.

* Let a friend know when you have finished and if possible celebrate together. If you are using it as part of your emotional healing after a hurt, a ceremonial ripping, burial or burning of few 'significant' items can work wonders. You will find yourself itching to move on to the next chapter of your life.

Surround yourself with stirring symbols

During the recession, my husband was becoming very stressed by the pressure he was under from major clients to make cuts in his prices that his business could not afford. Not surprisingly, my verbal reminders about how important it was to stay cool and assertive and not bow to unfair pressure were falling on very deaf ears. So instead, I bought him a very cute and patiently carved ancient mini Chinese tiger. I suggested that he keep it hidden in a pocket of his suit as a symbolic reminder of his need to stay calm and strong in the face of economic bullying. He was amused and used it. Now that he is back on his usual assertive track, the little tiger sits in my consultation room and is there to help anyone who needs a similar reminder.

Symbols are powerful motivators. They can communicate an inspirational message at high speed and with emotional impact. They can say in seconds something that might take many minutes or even hours to convey with words. So they are particularly useful when time is short, or concentration for reading or listening is elusive. And isn't this so often the case when you are battling through difficult patches in your life?

You could, of course, choose to use one of the many well-known archetypal symbols, such as a horse for power or a dove for peace. But for personal inspiration it is better to think of your own, as it will have much more emotional power for you. Here are some very different examples that have helped others and which I hope will inspire you to think of one you could use:

* A pressed sunflower – to recall a simple happy holiday in a French cottage to help get some perspective when Jane was worrying about money.

* Grandmother's brooch – a reminder for Charlie of his grandmother's resilience in the face of extreme hardship and uncertainty during the war.

* A mouse mat from Robben Island where Nelson Mandela was imprisoned – a reminder of how people can learn how to give up aggression and switch to negotiation and diplomacy to effect change (one of my own!).

* Photo of the presentation to Peter's son of a Duke of Edinburgh award for charity work – used to remind Peter of his son's great qualities a few years later when he was on remand for drug-related crimes.

* Certificate of final school exams – a reminder to Paula
that she had the intellectual capacity to pass the resit of
her university exam.

QUICK FIX: Transform possibilities into inspirational goals

Do you ever hear yourself starting a sentence with, 'I
suppose I could go/do/ ask . . . ' or, 'One day, I might
be able/try . . . ' or, 'I have thought of doing/saying/
saving for . . . '?

If so, and whenever you do, try to rephrase what
you're saying. See if you can transform your possibility into a goal. Smile as you speak, and make a
statement of intent by filling in the gaps in this
sentence: 'No, I am going to rephrase that. On . . .
[date] . . . I will [action] . . . and then I will reward
myself by . . . [treat].'

As soon as you can, commit your 'action plan' to
paper. Then share your intention with as many friends
as you can. This will increase your chances of achieving
success. I have found that many people leave off the
treat at the end. Try not to do that though, as planning
a reward for yourself will increase your motivation, as
well as giving you an additional morale boost.

If you leave your symbols around in the background of
your life, they will be repeatedly absorbed into your
subconscious mind along with the good feeling they

trigger. It is also a good idea to keep your symbols in public view whenever you can. People are then likely to comment on them, and each time this happens, even if you don't choose to explain its personal significance, you will be reminded of it and receive an internal uplift. It could also give you an opportunity to share your goal or dream with more people who will probably become additions to your supportive team of encouragers.

I would guess that many of you will have some kind of money worries weighing on your mind, simply because so many setbacks have either direct or indirect implications on financial resources. Even if your main source of income is not directly threatened, the cost of dealing with your problems may be worryingly high – fees for lawyers, estate agents, medical practitioners or undertakers, for example. Or you may need extra smaller sums to cover increased travel, takeaway or restaurant meals, stationery and books for information. And in the heat of a problem situation, people often (understandably) spend less discriminately, so that debts accrue more rapidly.

It is not unusual to try and push money worries to the back of your mind. My builder told me, with a laugh, only yesterday that during the last recession he used to throw his bills straight in the bin. He may find this memory funny now, but I am sure that at the time he didn't. He was probably so deep in despair or filled with anger that he behaved in this way because he felt powerless to improve his financial situation.

When you feel helpless like this, your morale and mood can sink to their lowest depths. Research undertaken by a new charity in the UK called FairBanking (see Resources, p. 265) has revealed that there is a strong correlation between wellbeing and the extent to which you have control over your finances. And this is exactly why I've included this short section on the subject, with expert input from FairBanking's director, Antony Elliott.

The tips here may not solve the major problems that are at the root of your worries, but they will boost your morale because you will feel more in control of some important aspects of your financial health. This section also has some ideas that could help you to make some real savings. You could then afford little treats to keep you motivated or maybe some extra help with services that might lessen the drain on your time and energy.

> *Money is better than poverty, if only for financial reasons.*
> **Woody Allen, comedian and film director**

Keep feelings and finances apart

Emotional decision-making (i.e. responding according to the guidance from your 'gut feelings') may work well in some areas of your life, but it should never be allowed to take any control in the management of your finances. This is especially so during difficult times when your emotional temperature is running hot and there is a danger that your feelings will get the better of you.

Your fear, for example, could make you too risk-averse and this might cause you to overly restrict your spending and suffer unnecessary inconvenience and insufficient uplifting treats. Or, on the other hand, your emotional state could lead you into doing just the opposite with even worse consequences. You're bound to have heard someone who was going through a rough patch say something like the following; or maybe even have said it yourself: 'What the hell – in for a penny, in for a pound; things can't get any worse, so what does it matter? I know it's a lot of money, but let's go for it.'

If you are in the position of needing the comfort of some financial cushioning, or you need to acquire extra resources, make sure that you defuse your feelings before doing any financial planning or decision-making. (Remember all those tips in Section 3?)

The emotional brain doesn't just understand things like interest rates or debt payments or finance charges.
Jonah Lehrer, author of *The Decisive Moment – How the Brain Makes Up Its Mind*

QUICK FIX: Get greener

Going greener can save you loads of money, as well as benefitting the planet. So why not ease your budget while easing your conscience? A guaranteed winner for your morale! Make this quick and easy to do by logging on to Friends of the Earth (see Resources, p. 265) – they can send you a tip a day by email or text.

 ## Have three personal budgets instead of one

Let's assume you do already have a current budget for your personal finances as they stand now. This means that you will only need to create an extra two. Unless your financial situation changes dramatically (for the worse or for the better), you may never actually need to use either of the budgets I suggest you now draw up. The purpose of doing them is purely psychological.

Your second budget, the 'survival budget', will help you to contain your financial fears, while the third, the 'hopeful budget', should give you an injection of optimism. It will remind you that things could improve financially for you even though you may find this difficult to believe right now. After all, none of us can be totally sure which way our fortunes may travel.

The survival budget

This should be a worst-case scenario forecast. It is particularly important to do if your income and savings are in danger of being drastically reduced as a result of your difficulties. It will help you to ease your worries.

So for each essential expense heading in your budget, put in a figure that is the minimum amount of money that you would require in order to meet that need without harming your own health or your family's (if you are supporting them). You should find the grand total is reassuring; it usually is for most people. If it is not, and if it scares you, start a 'rainy-day' savings plan straight away. I have been through many financially frightening times and am always surprised and delighted by how useful sums of money can be accumulated through simple ideas, such as having savings jars for different kinds of coin.

Just before the current global financial crisis hit, my husband and I had started planning a special holiday, but on learning that my pension would now be drastically depleted, I felt panic. To cheer myself up, I bought a cheap savings box in the shape of a fat cow. The cow now sits on the worktop in our kitchen and my husband and I goad each other into 'feeding' her from time to time. Of course, our cash cow's real value is not monetary but psychological.

She serves as a humorous reminder to keep a sense of perspective. After all, even if we end up camping we will still have our holiday.

The hopeful budget

This is the best-case scenario. Imagine that you are going to have a substantial increase in your income. Now, for each non-essential category, increase the amount you have allocated in your current budget. Make sure that you add in an amount for some motivating luxury treats for rewards and celebrations. Then read my next tip! It may help you acquire some of these, even if your circumstances stay much the same for a while.

 # Save for spectacular spending

In the area in Spain where we have a house, weddings tend to be very large events. Very often 500 guests are invited, even if families are on very low incomes, and traditionally, no expense is spared by either the host or the guests, who buy glamorous outfits and generous presents.

One wedding I went to in the midst of the major international financial crisis of 2009 was, however, a very different affair. The young couple, like the majority of their friends, were highly anxious about the very likely prospect of losing their jobs; just a quarter of the usual number of people was invited, although those of us selected were still treated to a luxurious feast. At the end of the meal, I was moved to see my young friends open a present from a large group of their friends. It was a small china piggy bank with their names and these words written on it: 'In these times of crisis, this is what we have saved. Congratulations!'

The bride was moved to tears and, of course, so was I (as I am once again as I write this)!

When I first drafted this book, I had in mind for this tip the creation of a special savings plan, the purpose of which would be to provide resources to give yourself a special treat, such as a weekend break. During difficult times it is harder than ever to prioritise such luxuries, even though you may know you desperately need them.

I would still suggest you create this kind of saving fund for treats, but my young friends' wedding gift was a wonderfully different example of spectacular 'spending'. It made me think that slowly accumulating enough money to be able to give someone a generous and unexpected gift could provide both the giver and the receiver with great morale boosts.

> *You make a living by what you get. You make a life by what you give.*
> **Winston Churchill, British Prime Minister (1940–45 and 1951–55)**

 # Be braver about borrowing what you can return

Before using this tip, you will need to edit out any negative messages about borrowing that are circling around on your hard drive. In the UK culture that I was brought up in we received many strong directives against both borrowing and lending, summed up by the proverb, 'Who goes a borrowing, goes a sorrowing', and Shakespeare's much-quoted, 'Never a borrower or a lender be'.

Of course, neither lenders nor borrowers should engage with people they mistrust, and they should be aware that there is a slight risk involved in this kind of transaction, especially if you are borrowing money. But I am suggesting that, in the main, you borrow goods and appliances more freely from friends and neighbours. As long as you know you can – and will – return what has been loaned, and you are fully prepared to be a lender too, there are many advantages to be had from being braver about borrowing. And during hard times the argument is even stronger. Here are some reasons why:

* You offer people an easy way to help you. I believe that the vast majority of people do want to help others who have problems. They may not offer help because they don't want to interfere or embarrass you, or they may simply be too shy or too busy to notice you need help. My experience is, however, that when you do ask people if they could lend you something you need, they are only too willing, and even appear to get pleasure from helping.

* By asking to borrow, you make it much easier for others to ask a favour from you. So you are likely to encounter another self-esteem-building opportunity.

* Although borrowing when you are in need can some-times feel a little humbling, it can be positive in that it

keeps your feet on the ground by reminding you that you do need some interdependence with others.

* When two people enter into a borrowing-lending 'contract', trust between them must come into play. This brings people closer together and usually they become more mutually supportive.

* It makes financial sense to borrow rather than buy something you would rarely use.

* It is more ecologically sound to share the use of something that costs the environment to produce.

If you are still nervous about asking to borrow, here are three tips to make it easier:

* Give the lender an easy escape route, by saying something like: 'Please feel free to say no; I am sure that I can ask someone else.' Or, 'I can manage fine without it, but I thought I would ask in case you could lend it to me. It would just make it easier to/be quicker than . . . '

* Specify the time when you will return or pay for what you have borrowed.

* Indicate your willingness to lend in return by saying something like, 'Of course, if there is ever anything you need or want to borrow, please don't hesitate to ask me.'

Here are a few suggestions of things you could borrow to save you money and strengthen your friendships and relationships with neighbours:

* CDs, DVDs and books: make a list for your friends and colleagues of those you have to lend and ask others to

do the same. Or invite your neighbours for coffee and a mutual browse at books for borrowing.

* Appliances: many of these are used very irregularly, such as long ladders, paint-strippers, spare tables and chairs, put-me-up beds and power hoses.

* Clothes: especially those expensive outfits that you may only use for one-off occasions; most people are flattered by this kind of request.

* Baby equipment: I recall very happily lending my crib out seventeen times in the three years before I needed it again myself.

* A home for a holiday: nowadays, most people and families have contacts scattered around the world. You could suggest a home exchange that would give both parties an interesting weekend or holiday break. Or, if you know someone with a second home, they may be willing to have friends stay there – this is a good way for the property to be checked and aired and usually it strengthens contact with the neighbours.

* Cars: some people have second cars sitting around doing very little, or they may not use their car during the week. You may be willing to come to a borrowing arrangement that includes an attractive 'share-the-expenses' deal for them, but would still save you lots of money. Alternatively, you could consider the setting up of a neighbourhood or company car pool. Or you could suggest an exchange of lifts to the supermarket or school to save on petrol.

*One of the best ways to do yourself a favour is to
lend somebody else a helping hand.*
Anonymous

QUICK FIX: Swap services
to save and give support

Think of services you could offer to your friends,
neighbours and colleagues. This could be a professional skill, such as fixing leaks if you are a plumber,
for example, or a personal talent, such as making delicious, nutritious soups if you cook well. Distribute the
list of services which you can offer, together with a
brief note about why you want to start a swap-services
scheme. Wait and see what happens. It'll cost you
nothing but an hour of your time, and it could save
you and your friends a considerable sum of money.

 # Do a deal with yourself over debt

I am writing this book in the depths of the most serious
recession in my lifetime, and one that most pundits
attribute largely to mismanaged financial debt. So this
subject is very much in the spotlight for me personally and
for people with whom I am currently working. Depression

is reported to be escalating fast, which indicates, yet again, the added psychological pressures that financial worries can bring.

Antony Elliott, the director of FairBanking (see p. 179), has made a special study of how people get into debt and how they get out of it; he told me that he has absolutely no doubt that levels of morale play a significant part: 'When morale is low, people tend to adopt a head-in-the-sand approach to their finances and debt. This is very concerning because we know from our research that anxiety increases in direct proportion to our debt/income ratio.'

So even if you are reading this during a financial boom period, if your morale is low it could still be useful to consider ways to ensure you don't get into trouble with debt. After all, no one ever knows when their financial fortunes may change, and doing anything that will add to your overall sense of security and independence is guaranteed to give you a boost.

Here are some ideas for deals you could do with yourself right now:

* Keep your head well out of the sand and never just sit back and hope that 'something will turn up'. Always respond to even a threat of financial difficulty by making some adjustment to the way you are managing or spending your money.

* Vow only to use cash or debit cards. Ceremoniously cut up your credit cards (or at least all but one of them, which you can keep locked away). Put the cut-up cards in a jar on your kitchen worktop at home, so you can feel smug and virtuous each time you see them! I know

of one debt consultant who keeps such a jar on his desk; he insists that every new client adds theirs to his store before he will advise them.

* Ensure that all your regular commitments are paid by direct debit the day after your pay cheque enters your bank account. Alternatively, if you use Internet banking, you can easily arrange for a lump sum which will cover all your bills to be sent from your current account into a savings account that does not offer a tempting debit card. It will only take you a few minutes to set this account up to make regular electronic transfers on the due dates.

* Increase your debt repayments to the highest level you can afford.

* Never borrow money from anyone just to buy a bargain. Debt advisers say that is one of the worst financial sins. (And isn't it the most tempting one too?)

* Delete all emails and/or tear up letters immediately that are offering to 'buy' or 'sell on' your debts. They are guaranteed to make your financial worries escalate in the not-too-distant long term. Your morale will nose-dive when you realise that you have allowed yourself to be duped.

And finally, two top tips from Antony Elliot:

* Do two monthly checks: the first is on your level of expenditure, to check that it is in line with your current means; the second is on your debt/income ratio, to ensure that it is still within your means.

* Think of your money as a series of pots. Imagine that you have a finite pot of money for each of your main expenditure zones and aim to stay within your budget for each. (This is particularly helpful for young adults when they are in the early stages of learning about budgeting.)

> *Debt is the slavery of the free.*
> **Publilius Syrus, Roman author, first century BC**

QUICK FIX: Spend to save on an expert

If you feel you could benefit from some sound financial advice right now, you might want to consider paying for a one-off meeting with a financial adviser. It may well be worth the cost of the consultation if it helps you to make significant savings in the long term. Do to take care to ensure that he or she is truly independent though, and not an insurance salesperson in disguise, as many are.

If you cannot afford to do this, think of investing some time, rather than money, in obtaining some free advice. This often entails queuing, if you go to a government or charitable agency. But there are plenty of ways you can use this waiting time productively, so it does not have to be a depressing experience. You could, for example, use the time for planning (see pp. 260–2), learning something new (see pp. 142–5) or meditating (see pp. 120–3).

Strengthen Your Circle of Support

Your circle of support could, at different points, include family members, people from your social network, neighbours, work colleagues or just kind-hearted acquaintances from within your community. During difficult times, however, it is those people whom you regard as 'friends' on whom you will probably depend the most. They are the people with whom you have an emotional bond, and there is an understanding (often unspoken) that you will give each other support. Of course, such friends may also play a dual role in that they are also family members, colleagues or your next-door neighbour – they might even share your bed if you are lucky enough to count on your partner as a friend.

When it comes to getting quality support it helps to know exactly who these friends are, and how they might be able to help you. In normal day-to-day life, you don't have to think too much about your friendships; you can afford to just let them wax and wane, as new faces appear in your life and others are left behind. But in difficult times, you may find that your 'hotchpotch' circle of friends cannot provide you with the kind of support that you need. Even your very best and most willing friends have personality limitations, as well as restraints on their emotional reserves and possibly their time.

With this in mind, this section offers you tips that will help you to analyse your current circle of support and iden-tify its strengths and weaknesses and show you ways in which you can extend and fortify it.

Draw your support from your friends' special strengths

A friend in need is a friend indeed.
English proverb

Friends can be drawn from your family, your social circle and your colleagues. If you appreciate each person's special strengths and draw mainly on these you will receive much better support from them. This will also reduce the chances of being disappointed by some of your friends and losing out on the other benefits those friendships can bring.

The following exercise will help you to appraise the special strengths of each of your friends, after which you will be able to draw on support from them more efficiently and quickly.

I often find people are reluctant to do this exercise – they say it sounds like an overly calculating approach to friendship. I agree that it may feel a bit odd to 'categorise' the qualities of your friends because this is not something you would usually do formally (even though most of us do it informally through gossip, all the time). But it is now accepted practice to analyse personal strengths and aptitudes in the business world when assessing and selecting staff and collaborators to do a job, and also in the dating world when searching for a suitable partner. We do it in these fields because this kind of analysis works, so why not apply it to friendship too?

You should find that the exercise will also help you to give others better support. It raises your awareness of your own strengths and limitations in relation to friendship.

You will see that I have listed sixteen categories of friends below; each has a title that reflects their special strength in relation to a support role that you may need. Some friends will obviously be able to play a number of these roles quite adequately; but remember, some roles could possibly be played just as well or even more 'skilfully' by someone else. It is always a good idea to see if you can 'spread the load' before asking for the support you need. Even your very best or most caring friend has their limitations. This is why I suggest that you 'nominate' at least one person as a back-up for the roles which you think you would need the most.

The exercise may reveal some gaps in your friendship circle, but don't panic – the tip on pp. 204–8 is on the subject of how to find new friends!

Friendship support roles: checklist exercise

Look at the following list of sixteen roles that friends can play in order to offer support. Read it through first without making any mental or written notes. If you want to add one or more roles, feel free to do so.

Next, list the roles on a piece of paper or on your computer. Think about each one more carefully now in relation to the friends you have and note down their names beside any of the roles that they do or could fulfil for you.

1. The cheerful chatterers
They have a sunny disposition. You can always count on them to be smiling and they are never lost for words. Their

conversation is light and often predictable. They don't need explanations for everything and tend to take life as it comes. They are relaxing and easy to be with.

2. The old timers

They share a good deal of history with you and love to look back at the old days. They help you to remember the young you and the you who has survived life's ups and downs. Conversation with them brings you a 'Mum's cooking' kind of glow that is comforting and boosts your self-esteem.

3. The adventurers

They always have something new and interesting to tell you about their lives. They encourage you out of your comfort zone, and get you excited about doing something new.

4. The caring listeners

They will listen patiently to you, with genuine interest and without interruptions and unwanted advice. You feel better after talking to them, even though you may be no nearer a solution.

5. The devil's advocates

These are the friends who always seem to come up with an opposite point of view. They may do this just because they get a kick out of arguing and debating. This can be useful because they can help you to understand others better, especially when your feelings are intense and could be blinding you in some way. Also, your arguments with them can help you to firm up your views and decisions and make you more determined and able to put forward your ideas or case more convincingly.

6. The clowns

You can always count on them to see the funny side of a black situation. Having a laugh with them is very relaxing and sometimes enlightening. They can also be great for taking you down a peg or two if you have become a bit blinded to your own faults and limitations.

7. The thinkers

These are very sensible friends. They are especially good to talk to when a situation is complicated or emotionally charged. They will help you to weigh up the pros and cons before taking any action. This can save you acting hastily and repenting later. These friends are also good to talk to when you'd like to take your mind off your problems for a while. They love discussions which involve finding solutions to any kind of issue or problem. Talking with them is like doing a workout on your mind; it will distract you from your problems, while at the same time making your mental muscles stronger.

8. The doers

These are not the best listeners in the world, but if you need some practical help you can count on them to get cracking without delay. They often need some guidance from you about what needs doing as they are doers rather than thinkers, but they usually get a great buzz out of being needed, so don't hold back from asking.

9. The SOS rescuers

These are your truly 'cool' friends, in that they keep their heads in a crisis. Indeed, they are often at their best during tough times. Even if they are not very practical themselves, you can count on them to have a long list of useful telephone numbers and contacts.

10. The soldiers

These friends will stand up for you when you may not be capable of fighting your own corner. They are super-assertive, and even prepared to be aggressive when they see a great injustice being done. They have good stamina and persistence, so you can count on them to be around for longer than others. They are also good at getting an 'army' of support together from their own contacts to give you even more back-up.

11. The financiers

These friends are great budgeters and always know where the bargains and good deals can be found. They are great if you need some extra money. Some may be more than happy to help out with some extra no-strings-attached money. Others may be able to offer 'safe' advice on loans that will not burden you with a debt you cannot truly afford.

12. *The visionaries*

These are great people with whom to talk through your dreams and hopes. They will often encourage you to think 'big' and take a long-term perspective. This means that they are very good people to take to lunch if you are obsessing about too many of today's little problems or have been stuck in the same rut for too long.

13. *The inspirational survivors*

These friends don't need to *do* anything in particular to help you. They have already done their bit by having faced and come through difficult challenges. Their strength is that they are a living example to you of how you could become stronger (and even nicer!) as a result of tough times. So in order to give you support they just need to be themselves and be a presence in your life. Simply talking about the weather with them can remind you of their inspirational story and be enough to give you a boost of courage and confidence.

14. *The competitive companions*

These people make goal-getting fun. They are always willing to challenge you to have a go against them. You don't have to worry about damaging their confidence as they are great losers as well as winners. Competing with them in any kind of way will help you to extend your potential and so increase your confidence.

15. The people-readers

These are the friends who not only read other people's minds but yours too! They can be very good at seeing through your self-defensive waffle, even when you can't. They can help you to understand why people may have acted in a certain way or said things which puzzle or enrage you. Also, if they are people you know you can trust, you can have some satisfying character assassination sessions with them! This can help you to let off steam after you have had to take some stick from people who have upset or bullied you.

16. The soulmates

These are often referred to as 'best' friends. They know and understand you so well that you may not even need to speak before they know what's bothering you. You can count on their love for you whatever and whenever. Even though you may not have seen them for ages, your relationship slots back into the same place as soon as you meet again. You can always be yourself with them and know that your secrets and disclosures are safe. But, however special these friends are, they can never fulfil all the above roles; and, in times of crisis, they may be too shocked or emotional on your behalf to even be able to fulfil those they normally do well.

So in these difficult days, forget worrying about who is a 'true' friend and who isn't. Some friends may happen to have more to offer you at this point, while others may come into their own at another time. And remember, the

QUICK FIX: Deepen your key relationships

> *Soulmates are people who bring out the best in you. They are not perfect, but are always perfect for you.*
> **Anonymous**

Research has shown that you can instantly deepen your relationships with people you care most about by increasing any one of the following five factors (but why not go for the whole package as soon as you can?):

1. Time   3. Sharing   5. Fun
2. Touch   4. Caring

As a mum whose daughter is on the other side of the world, I can't instantly increase the 'touch' factor, but I have found video calling is a very satisfying second best. And, if you're as soppy as I am, you can always touch the screen!

Strengthening your soulmate relationships should always be a high priority. These people may not be able to fulfil many of the support roles you need right now, but you can count on them to be at your side come rain or shine.

> *When it hurts to look back, and you're scared to look ahead, you can look beside you and your best friend will be there.*
> **Anonymous**

support that a friend can give you in your hour of need is not necessarily a reflection of how good that person is or is not. Nor is it an indication of the degree of love they have for you. Sometimes, your nearest and dearest are useless in a crisis and it can be the neighbour you hardly speak to who becomes your star support.

 ## Fill in the supportive friendship gaps

If a man does not make new acquaintances as he advances through life, he will soon find himself alone. A man should keep his friendships in constant repair.
Samuel Johnson, author

You may think that you don't have the time or energy to go out seeking new friends right now. But if you have done the exercise on pp. 197–202 you will find this task much easier than you think because it will give you a clear idea of the specific qualities you are looking for in friends.

However, it will also help you greatly if you develop new friendships in a steady, step-by-step way. Of course, there will be exceptions, as there are to every rule, and occasionally we seem to 'click' straight into a deep relationship at step one. Generally though, it is wise to play friendship-building safely and slowly, especially when you are in a stressed and, therefore, a possibly vulnerable state.

Use the following steps as a guide, only moving on from one to the next if the last one has gone well. If it hasn't, it is unlikely that this is the kind of person you need as a friend right now, and it's easier to extract yourself at an early stage of a relationship than to wait until expectations and habits and emotional connections have been firmly established.

Step 1

Increase your opportunities to make very general safe 'small talk' to become more familiar with each other.

Step 2

Encourage topics of conversation and questions which you think will reveal the person's attitudes, beliefs and aptitudes, especially to problem situations.

Step 3

Suggest ways to strengthen your connection with each other by doing something that feeds an interest or need you both share. This could be, for example, going to see a film or watch a match together. Or, if you are from different countries, but both have an interest in food and cooking, you could suggest that you each prepare a meal that is typical of your cultures.

Step 4

Start to be more self-revealing. (Note that this self-disclosure step comes before you start to ask them personal questions.) Share something about your likes and dislikes, hopes and dreams.

Step 5

If they show willingness to share, encourage them to talk more revealingly about their plans and hopes and problems in relation to achieving these. But always be sensitive to any signs of reluctance. You can have a great friendship with someone even though you are not equally self-revealing. A much more important key to friendship success is that each person feels that their needs and personality is respected by the other.

Step 6

Try to find a way to help them. This could be by giving them a useful contact, or by passing on some information from a newspaper or a website you found, for example. Alternatively, you could offer to do something practical for them. Make it clear that your help comes with no strings attached.

Step 7

Share more about your own difficult situation that might reveal your needs. If all is going well with the development of your relationship, your new friend will almost certainly offer to help in some way; and when they do, you should accept it, whatever it is. A mutual exchange of help is one of the greatest ways to move a relationship forward.

If your new friend can't help you right now, they should let you know that they are sorry about not being able to support you. And they should indicate that there is a good reason why this is so at the moment. For your friendship to progress, you don't need to have immediate help from them. Nor do you need to know why they can't currently offer support, but you do need to feel that they would be there to support you either emotionally or practically if they could be.

Step 8

The next time your friend offers help or you want to ask them for support, try to ensure that you receive the kind that fits with your needs (i.e. the current gaps in your supportive friendship). If their offer isn't a good match and you think they could offer some other kind of help, say something like this: 'Actually, I already have a couple of people who babysit, but I know you used to work in a bank. I wouldn't mind a bit of advice about . . . '

> *There isn't much that I can do, but I can share an hour with you, and I can share a joke with you . . . as on our way we go.*
> **Maude V. Preston, writer**

Where can you find new supportive friends?

In the main there are three kinds of opportunities to extend your social network:

* You can get to know some of your existing acquaintances better, seeking out those, for example, whom you know have also been through a tough time and appear to have come through it well.

* You could be more proactive about starting up conversations with 'likely suspects' who you come across on your course through life. Always be on the lookout for

interesting bits of information and news that will provide safe small-talk openers. If, for example, you travel a good deal on trains, you could prepare some talking points by doing an Internet search for interesting comparative statistics on rail travel in different regions or countries. This kind of information would have the added bonus of lifting everyone's spirits should you be on an overcrowded train or caught in a hold-up together.

Always take care not to probe with questions on sensitive subjects, such as religion, politics or family. And it should go without saying that personal comments are a big no–no as conversation-openers.

* Ask your existing friends and contacts to introduce you to any of their friends or contacts who fit with the qualities you are looking for. A good example is that of Gill, a single mother, whose son, Rob, was being charged with possession of a drug. Gill knew that a cousin of one of her friends was a drug counsellor. She managed to arrange to get herself invited to the pub where the drug-counselling team socialised after work, and there she began a friendship with a woman who was very supportive when Rob's case came to court.

Back off sensitively from morale-drainers

A true friend knows your weaknesses but shows you your strengths; feels your fears but fortifies your faith; sees your anxieties but frees your spirit; recognises your disabilities but emphasises your possibilities.
William Arthur Ward, writer

This sums up very well the qualities of morale-boosting friends. Morale-drainers are their direct opposites. At best, they are overly self-focused, will more or less ignore you, or take you for granted; while at worst, they may know your strengths, but remind you constantly of your weaknesses; they can be insensitive about your fears, disappointments and sadness and they may be disrespectful about your beliefs. When you are with them or have just left them, you can sense that your hope and self-confidence are deflated. And, to make matters worse, you usually also feel physically tired and too apathetic around them to do anything, let alone rise to your own defence!

First rule: let yourself off the hook. Because you are going through a rough patch yourself, this is not the time to either confront them or feel sorry for them.

The second rule is to back off as fast as you can. A few white lies to use as excuses are, in my opinion, quite justified. But make sure they are ones where you won't be caught out. The best advice I can give here is to provide them with the minimum of information.

So when they are talking and you feel you need to back off, you can say briefly and quickly: 'Sorry to interrupt, but I have a dinner date. I must go immediately. Take care and have a good evening. Bye.' Don't get involved with long explanations, such as: 'I'm very sorry to interrupt. It is not that I don't want to listen; it's just that I'm meeting Margaret in a minute – we are having dinner. She is having a hard time since her husband had that affair and I really mustn't be late. So sorry to have to break off our conversation. But you know me; I'm always in a rush. We'll catch up again next week, perhaps. You know where I am if you need me.'

The latter gives the morale-drainer lots of unnecessary information which can prompt questions. It also is over-apologetic and even includes a self-put-down, ending with an attempt to soften 'the blow' by inviting another date for a catch-up. All these are common mistakes. At first, you may feel it is rude to be brief. But it's not; it is simply being assertive and setting boundaries.

An alternative, super-assertive way of handling this situation is to be even more direct and say something like: 'Sorry, I'm finding it hard to concentrate. I'm switching off because I don't want to get depressed. I have to look after number one right now. It would be best if you could find someone else to talk to about this. I hope you will understand that I have to say goodbye now. Take care.'

But don't forget – the first example I gave is good enough. Don't you have a right to protect yourself from morale-drainers? It's to no one's advantage to have yet another depressed person in the world!

QUICK FIX: Organise food-sharing feasts

> *Of all the things that wisdom provides to help one live one's entire life in happiness, the greatest by far is the possession of friendship. Eating or drinking without a friend is the life of a lion or a wolf*
>
> **Epicurus, philosopher**

Anthropologists think that the very first social activity that primitive man created was the shared meal. Ever since then, in every corner of the globe, communal feasting has been used to create and cement friendships.

At this moment in time, you may be too busy, tired, sad or broke to cook for your friends, so arranging the kind of feast to which everyone brings a dish could be the answer. I always find that there is delicious food at these events, because people usually bring along their best dish. Also, it gives people the option not to cook unless they want to do so. If you offer to host the occasion, you can provide the water, tea and coffee so you won't need to cook anything.

Invest more time in your community

The best portion of a good man's life – his little nameless acts of kindness, unremembered acts of kindness.
William Wordsworth, poet

One of the comments people most commonly make after a major disaster has hit a community is how it brought people together to help and comfort each other. More often than not, when I talk to people who are going through a private hell and ask them if there is anyone near by to whom they can turn for support, they cannot think of anyone they know well enough to ask. Admittedly, I do most of my work in London, but I understand that this phenomenon is not exclusive to large, metropolitan areas.

I have moved house too many times in my life to be able to keep count. As a result, I have become something of an expert at finding ways to become quickly integrated into communities. Offering to volunteer to help with or initiate a community project has been, for me, one of the quickest and most satisfying ways in.

In my experience, it pays to think and plan before rushing in to help with the first project you encounter or are requested to help with. In order to obtain the best return in terms of helping the community, while at the same time boosting your own morale, you will need to bear several things in mind.

Research and respect local needs

You can do this by asking neighbours and meeting leaders of local organisations. It also helps to spend time reading the local newspaper and listening to any local radio station. You may have to put your passionate desire to be part of a book group on the back burner if all anyone else wants to talk about at the moment is how to prevent building work on their green belt.

Try to match a local need or interest to one of your talents

If you are a good organiser, you could offer to put on trips for the residents' association, or be on the committee of a charity or pressure group. If your talent is writing, you could perhaps, offer to start a newsletter. If you have years of driving experience, you could join the pool of car drivers for the local hospice. Playing to your strengths will be much more satisfying for you and make your involvement much more effective.

Under- rather than over-commit

This is much easier said than done (over-commitment is one of my weaknesses!). Every community and charitable project is run on shoestrings and is constantly thirsty for help. It is particularly hard to say no in crises, but remember – these are inevitable and frequent in this world. So you have to be clear about the commitment you can give, and stick within your capability boundaries with super-assertiveness. Remind yourself that over-commitment leads to resentfulness, bitterness and burnout – none of which will endear you to others or build your morale.

QUICK FIX: Strengthen your colleague support

> *It is an absolute bonus to make friends out of colleagues.*
> **Jennifer Aniston, actress**

Share as much of your load as you can with trustworthy colleagues. If it is not appropriate to give details of your problem, simply say something like: 'It is personal and I'd rather not talk about it, but I'm having a tough time at the moment.' By sharing in this limited way, you will almost always receive offers of extra support and be shown more understanding if you need time off or are having the odd 'off day'.

When you let colleagues know that you are having difficulties, try also, if possible, to give them something useful to do to help. For example, suggest that having the occasional drink or lunch together to talk about subjects other than your problems will help you. This will strengthen the friendship side of your relationship and make it more likely that they will support you in other ways should the need arise.

Network before you need to do so

Hundreds of surveys have been carried out to identify how people find jobs, and the story is always the same. In major surveys, between 43 and 89 per cent of job-seekers said that they secured their roles through networking. There is also evidence to suggest that when a job is found this way, the job-holder is more likely to fit better into the organisational culture, have a shorter learning curve, perform to a higher degree and stay in the job longer than someone who enters the company via another route.

'No, I don't do networking . . . I've never needed to do so. I have always hated it. I'm just not that kind of person. I wouldn't know where to start, and I'm really bad at that sort of thing. Small talk is not my scene. I'm the kind of person who is always stuck in a corner with some sad person if ever I am at a social event.'

This is what John, a fifty-four-year-old executive who had just been made redundant, said at his exit interview. And his attitude is far from unusual. My husband, who works in the career-transition business, hears this kind of reaction frequently when he suggests that networking would help. And I hear similar reactions when I am helping people to move on from personal setbacks; my clients may need to network socially to find a new partner after a divorce or bereavement or need to find new friends because they have had to move home or they have fallen out irreparably with their best friend.

Many people think they are simply too busy to network and that they cannot justify putting it on their priority list until they are in desperate need of more contacts. But very often, the real reason is that they, like John, dread the thought of doing it. This may be especially true in the UK because we are a shy culture, but I have also heard many people admit to the same problem in southern Spain, where on the surface everyone appears to be much more socially confident and outgoing.

A good network, whether it is for your business or social life, should be an interactive web of people who are mutually trusting and also have a commitment to be mutually helpful. Building up such a network is a long-term project. If you move in too quickly and try to use an already established network for help before you have proved yourself to be trustworthy and helpful, you may meet a few 'cold shoulders'. And that is one of the most common reasons why people become disillusioned with networking.

Another reason why people give up on networking is that they don't enjoy the experience. When you explore the reasons for this, it almost always boils down to a lack of confidence in managing the social scene. Like John, they often say a networking event was 'a waste of time' or 'boring' because they always get 'stuck' with certain people. This, along with so many social-skill difficulties, can easily be put right.

Once you have learnt and practised the tricks of the networking trade, anyone can do it. You don't have to be a certain personality type. Introverts and extroverts may have different styles but they can be equally successful. The skills you need for networking socially or for work are more or less the same. Here is a plan for getting you into immediate networking action:

1. Put networking on your to-do list.

2. Review the networks you have already and choose three relationships to nurture more deeply right now.

3. Make an action plan for doing the above.

4. Set a goal for making at least one new contact a month. This could be through joining an established network or just striking up conversations with people you don't know at work, on the bus/train/plane, at the school gate or in the gym. I suggest that you aim to have had a follow-up meeting or a chat on the phone or over a coffee with each person within a month.

5. Buy or borrow a book on networking for tips and advice or book yourself in for a workshop.

6. If you know a great networker, offer to buy them lunch in exchange for giving you some advice. Their wisdom could save you loads of time and disappointments.

7. Make a pledge to ensure that for the time being, when networking, you are not going to be seeking help. Your focus will be simply on getting to know other people and letting them get to know you.

8. Make another pledge to find a way to help someone in your network at least once every two weeks. This could be offering advice or passing on a contact.

9. Buy a very small book in which you can record your networking activities and new contacts and take it around with you wherever you go. Alternatively, if you

use computers or a mobile phone for making notes, create a file called 'Networking' immediately!

10. Check that you are enjoying your networking. If you are not, you will not be successful. If you are finding it hard-going, it is highly likely that you are not doing something right. You may need to adjust your action planning and target areas. You may need to brush up on some skills. Or, perhaps you need to change your style and network in a way that is more suited to your personality or your specific needs. For example you may find one-to-one encounters much more enjoyable and satisfactory than party gatherings (or vice versa).

For more help, check out a book written by my husband (who runs masterclasses in networking) and myself – a self-help guide which addresses most common difficulties in this area: *Confident Networking for Career Success and Satisfaction* (see Resources, p. 265).

SECTION 9
Stand Up to Sabotage

Throughout this book we have examined how people tend to sabotage their own recovery. We have acknowledged, for example, that many of us do this by not taking good enough care of our stressed bodies and minds, by letting ourselves sink into negative thinking or by holding back when it comes to asking for the support we need. But there are, of course, many different ways in which **others** can sabotage your recovery process, and the tips in this section focus on preventing this from happening.

Most of the time, in my experience, people who do this, do so unintentionally, but you may occasionally meet people who do it deliberately. Either way, it should be stopped. But when you are also trying to deal with many other difficulties, it is sometimes easier to just let it wash over you. The trouble with doing this, however, is that passively 'giving in' depresses your morale. You can feel even more victimised if you've already had a raw deal, you can feel even more useless if you've been rejected and you can become even more despairing if you have encountered a serious disappointment or loss.

The tips in this section will help you to be self-protective without getting into de-energising fights. Taking assertive action will definitely improve your self-confidence and morale and could improve your relationship with your 'saboteur' as well. This is particularly true if someone has been trying to help you, but has been doing so in a way that is wrong for you.

Remind yourself of your personal rights

It is amazing to me how, in very difficult problem situations, even truly nice people can become critical, arrogant, know-alls and interfering busy-bodies. Often, their intentions are very well meaning, but their interference and dogmatic advice are not helpful. This could be because you are not ready to take the action they suggest, or you want to try doing it in your own way, even if it might not work out right.

I admit that I too can become one of those people, when someone I care about deeply is in distress. My horrible, bossy side takes over from my nurturing one. Luckily, my family are assertive enough to tell me to back off, but less confident friends will unfortunately tend to just go quiet on me. With a few sad exceptions, I can now spot this happening. But this wasn't always the case. Before going through many years of personal and professional development training, I didn't have enough self-awareness and sensitivity to spot emotional clues from others to stop this sabotaging behaviour from damaging relationships.

Perhaps you have already encountered this kind of annoying hindrance from others. If so, I hope you have managed to give them the 'back-off' message. But if you find that difficult to do, you may first need to firm up your belief in your rights to do this.

The exercise below will help you to fix your personal rights in your memory, after which you should find that when you encounter sabotaging behaviour, one or more of these rights will instantly spring into your mind. Some people say that it is like having a guardian angel (or me!) sitting on their shoulder, reminding them to stand up for themselves.

How to deal with saboteurs

* Read through the list below and tick those rights that relate most to you and your situation. Make a note in your mind or on paper of how they can be disrespected in your everyday life; remember that people can be disrespectful of your rights even though they may be motivated by the very best intentions (the 'I-was-only-trying-to-help' syndrome).

* Personalise this list of rights by adapting, adding or subtracting rights.

* Write down your own personal rights list and read it out loud at least once every day for a week.

✔ I have the right to do things my way.

✔ I have the right to make my own decisions and cope with the consequences.

✔ I have a right to make mistakes.

✔ I have a right to not be a perfect person.

✔ I have a right to privacy.

✔ I have a right not to know about or understand something.

✔ I have a right to change my mind.

✔ I have a right to be alone sometimes.

✔ I have a right to take time to heal and recover.

✔ I have a right to feel what I feel.

✔ I have a right to refuse help that I don't think I need.

✔ I have a right to express my feelings in a controlled way.

✔ I have a right to be treated as an individual.

✔ I have a right to ask for help, even though I may be refused.

✔ I have a right to choose who I want to be with.

✔ I have a right to move on at my own pace.

✔ I have a right to be positive and optimistic.

✔ I have a right to seek professional help if I choose.

✔ I have a right to read self-help books!

Once you have firmly established these rights in your mind, you will be able to make good use of the rest of the tips in this section.

 # Smoke the vipers out of the nest

If someone is trying to rile you, use the simple assertiveness technique of 'fogging' to tip them off your back; this is a brilliant tactic for dealing with people who are intent on picking a fight. They back off instantly because it creates a kind of verbal smokescreen between you (hence its name)

and gives them the impression (though *not* correctly) that you have given in. It is far less stressful than giving them the fight they want.

Here's an example:

The viper: 'You brought this on yourself, you know. You married her . . . I told you she was no good for you.'

Your fogging response: 'You could be right. Perhaps I shouldn't have married her.'

The use of the words 'could' and 'perhaps' is where the smokescreen comes in. Swallow your wounded pride (you can always reboot your self-esteem later if you need to; see pp. 40–2). Just enjoy the satisfaction of seeing the viper lost for words! If you don't believe it works, practise it with a friend first.

 ## Say 'No' as though you mean it

When your morale is low, unless you are super-confident your ability to communicate in an assertive manner is almost always affected, so that you may often find yourself more open to being led into doing things that you would prefer not to do. Until you are feeling emotionally stronger, use these tips to help your 'No' to come across more powerfully:

* As soon as you hear the question or suggestion, move deliberately into a confident pose by either placing both feet on the ground and straightening your posture or sitting a little further forward.

* Use the trick of pausing before saying something important. In this moment, concentrate on taking at least one
slower and deeper breath. This will help to deepen your
voice and keep it steady.

* Catch the eye of the person before starting to speak. Or
you can look at their ear if you can't face direct eye
contact – it has the same effect!

* Don't give reasons for your refusal; they provide ammu-
nition for an argument for which you probably haven't
enough energy or confidence to win, so just stick with a
short, direct polite statement such as: 'No, I would
prefer not to do that today. But thank you for asking.'

* If they try and persuade you with a seductive plea, just
repeat the same statement, including an emphatic word
and leaving out the thanks. Trust that the repetition is
very important, even though it may sound parrot-like to
you at first: 'No, I *really* would prefer not to do that
today.'

* If they ask you what you are doing instead, don't tell
them. That again would offer them 'food' to argue that
what they are suggesting would be better. Simply say:
'It's nothing to do with anything I am doing, it's just that
I don't want to do that today.' By this time, they should
have got the message – if not, just persist with your
repetition until they do . . . and they will!

Politely push back put-downers

We are injured and hurt emotionally, not so much by other people or what they say, but by our own attitude and our own response.
Maxwell Maltz, self-help guru and author

Put-downs are a type of remark or behaviour that directly or indirectly disrespects one of your personal rights. They can sabotage you by deflating your self-confidence and motivation. Sometimes they are very hard to spot at the time they are given. But afterwards, you can feel a bit uncomfortable and irritated, even though the person appeared to be being nice.

1. Learn to quickly recognise and label put-down behaviour. The list of examples below will help.

2. Remind yourself of your appropriate right.

3. Give an assertive response without unnecessarily justifying your case or becoming overly defensive. It is a waste of postive energy to debate with a put-downer. But beware – they are good at provoking an argumentative response.

If you do not realise you have been put down until later, don't let your feelings fester and do nothing. Write down what was said and then compose an appropriate response. Practise saying your response out loud. You could talk through possibilities with an assertive friend and rehearse using role-play with them. Next time you will be sure to respond assertively.

Here are some common styles of put-downs and suggestions for an assertive response.

Prying

Example

'I know you said you don't want to talk about what happened, but can you just give me an idea of who was involved. Is it someone I know?'

Your right

You have the right to privacy.

Assertive response

'What happenned is still something I want to keep private.'

Nagging

Example

'Isn't it time you started looking for a new girlfriend?'

Your right

You have a right to move on at your own pace.

Assertive response

'When the time is the right for me, I'll get another girl-friend.'

Lecturing

Example

'You shouldn't just take the first job that is offered. You should take more account of the long-term prospects.'

Your right

You have the right to make your own decisions and cope with the consequences.

Assertive response

'I want to take this job. It could turn out to be the wrong choice, but if that happens, I'll deal with it.'

Questioning your choice

Example

'Are you sure you are making a wise choice to stay with him after he has deceived you so badly?'

Your right

You have a right to choose who you want to be with.

Assertive response

'I am making the right choice for me.'

Unwanted advice

Example

'I know two people who went to see therapists and both found the experience a waste of time and money. I think you have the guts to beat this on your own.'

Your right

You have a right to seek professional help if you choose.

Assertive response

'I have made the appointment and that's that.'

Insulting labels

Example

'You Easterners are so deferential to your elders. You shouldn't let your father determine your life.'

Your right

You have a right to be treated as an individual.

Assertive response

'I am an individual and so is my father. What other people from the East do is not relevant.'

 # Question your critics to make them constructive

Criticism may not be agreeable, but it is necessary. It fulfils the same function as pain in the human body. It calls attention to an unhealthy state of things.
Winston Churchill, British Prime Minister (1940–45 and 1951–55)

Instead of clamming up when criticism hits, empower yourself by calmly and confidently asking information-seeking questions. If your critic is capable of being constructive, this will usually bring forth some good suggestions. If your critic can't come up with an answer because, perhaps, they are in a bad mood and you were an easy target, this kind of questioning takes them aback. You will then find you have effectively stopped them in their critical tracks. So whatever their response, you are a winner.

Unless you have tried this kind of tactic before, it may seem very hard to do. But actually it just takes practice. Watch confident people use it, such as politicians when they are dealing with aggressive interviewers. They have probably been trained in this technique.

It is easy to train yourself and can be good fun to practise it with a friend. They can play the role of someone who you think really would like to take you down a peg or two. Even if you never get the opportunity to do this in real life, you will have had a good morale boost from just doing the rehearsal.

Questions to use with critics

1. Request specific details if they are generalising

* 'How many times have you noticed that I . . . ?'

* 'What do you actually hear me say or do?'

2. Request clarification if they are hinting

* 'Are you saying that I'm not capable of working yet?'

* 'Do you mean to say that I am lazy?'

* 'Do you think I am a hysteric and not really that heart-broken?'

3. *Request more criticism*

* 'Is there anything else you think I am doing wrong or could do better?'

* 'Is there anything else about my character that you don't like or irritates you?'

> *We don't criticise. Criticism is an enemy. You've got to make loving, positive suggestions.*
> **Dorothy Sarnoff, singer and pioneer of self-help**

QUICK FIX: Call in your army if the going gets too tough

Very often, setbacks require that you take on battles with dauntingly large organisations (such as social security systems or insurance companies with one-size-fits-all rules) or imposing authority figures (such as your child's opinionated head teacher when they've just failed their exams).

In these situations, or any others where you might be up against a first-class bully, don't hesitate to rally support. Bullying tactics require group force to out-manoeuvre them at the best of times.

Remember the friends you labelled 'the soldiers' on p. 200? They are the people to call on now. Perhaps if these weren't such hard times for you, you could manage on your own. But why not give yourself a break and use the extra support?

SECTION 10
Maintain Your Momentum

I n the immediate aftermath of a crisis, you often get a surge of energy, and the extra shot of adrenalin that your body creates helps to keep you going. However, the later 'moving-on' process can sometimes seem to drag on interminably, and it can be especially hard to keep going forward positively if you have little control over the outcome or when you have no idea as to how long a problem will take to resolve.

Even when you do have control over the goals and action plans that you set for yourself, the process of achieving them is rarely straightforward; you may already have found yourself feeling that your progress is one step forward and two steps back.

At the same time, you may find that you are starting to feel less supported by others. The initial rally of back-up from friends and family may well have receded by now, just at the time when your adrenalin charge has subsided, leaving you feeling overwhelmed and badly in need of reassurance and comfort.

If you are now at that point where you have to pick up the pieces of your old life or forge a new and challenging pathway, it's likely that you'll be feeling much more alone than you did earlier on in your crisis. It is now that you need to be able to draw on a 'tool-box' of self-help strategies to help you remain on or return to a positive course. The tips in this section will give you those tools; they will boost your spirits, calm your fears and eradicate some of the bad habits and stress that may be affecting your momentum. Finally, there is also an exercise that will help you to formulate a simple action plan and select your own three top tips from this book to kick-start you into action.

QUICK FIX: Focus on the 'why' when the 'how' gets tough

He who has a why to live, doesn't mind the how.
Nietzsche, philosopher

Find or make a pictorial representation of the light you can see (or want to see) at the end of your tunnel. For example, this could be:

* the joining of male and female hands (to represent a new partnership)

* the garden of your new home

* the logo of a major company – your new job

* a dove sitting on a map of your country (to indicate peace).

Underneath your picture, you could write Nietzche's wonderfully wise words, quoted above; then whenever the going appears to be getting too tough: look, read and digest.

Deal head-on with your worst-case scenario

Only the unknown frightens men. But once a man has faced the unknown, that terror becomes the known.
Antoine de Saint Exupery, author

Fear is undoubtedly one kind of motivator that can spur you into action. As long as you can control your fear though, you can use it positively to help keep you going (and that's almost certainly why it exists).

I have already suggested a strategy for coping with panic paralysis (see pp. 86–90) which is a great fear-buster. But here is another way which involves using your imagination to bring your worst fear out of the shadows so you can deal with it head-on. You can then rehearse ways to calm your heart's emotional response and prepare a constructive contingency plan to include practical actions that you can take immediately. Doing all this will put your mind at rest and enable you then to forget this worst-case scenario and get on with living positively for today and moving on in an optimistic way to the future.

1. Use a creative visualisation technique (by following the instructions on pp. 169–70) to create a picture of your worst-case scenario in your mind's eye. Alternatively, another way to achieve the same effect is to write your scenario out as a story. Use the present tense to bring it more to life. When you have finished it, read your story

Outline for a contingency plan

* Summary of feared outcome.
* Make a list of the specific impacts that this could produce in each of the following areas of your life:
  * Personal relationships and home life
  * Working life
  * Finances
  * Physical health
  * Emotional wellbeing
  * Social life
* Make a note of the names of the key people whom you could call to help and support you with these particular issues, or to support your dependants or loved ones, if you think there's a chance you will not be around. Ensure that you also have their contact details readily at hand.
* Note what action you (or others) could take to cope with this situation and deal with its effects in each of the relevant areas of your life. If you cannot think of anything you or others could do, ring a few of the support people you listed above for ideas. Trust that they will have the answers that either your fear or inexperience is stopping you from recognising.
* Test out any aspects of your plan that can be tested. For example, walk the escape route if you fear a fire or terrorist attack on a building you are in. Survivor

research has shown that this kind of testing increases your chances of surviving considerably.

* File this plan somewhere safe and, if you think this is necessary, inform others in your life where it can be found.

out loud as though it has just happened. You can do this on your own or with a friend. Either of these creative techniques should activate the fight/flight fear response in your body.

2. Use the breathing exercise on p. 89 to calm down your pulse if it has started to race. You could also use the mindfulness technique (pp. 98–9) to visualise your heart beating and pumping through your veins to slow it down to its normal rate.

3. Now that you are physically calm, write out a contingency plan for yourself using the outline opposite to ensure that you deal with the situation effectively and recover emotionally as well.

4. Note down the action you are going to take in the *immediate* future to ensure that your worst-case scenario does not become a reality.

    For example:

    ✔ I am going to eat and drink more healthily.

    ✔ I am going to network twice a week to increase my chances of getting a job as quickly as possible.

    ✔ I am going to take advice about managing my money better.

✔ I am going to disclose our family problem to one trusted friend for support. I am also going to seek advice from the substance abuse centre to see how best I can help my son.

✔ I am going to ensure that my mother does the brain exercises recommended by the Alzheimer's Society.

5. Note down any *immediate* action you could take to help others cope with the situation, if you fear you are not going to be around:

✔ Ring lawyer regarding revisions to my will.

✔ Ring my brother and talk through my fears and plans and give him the name of my lawyer.

✔ Set up a contingency savings fund.

✔ Contact the funeral directors and ask for funeral costings, etc. and set this money aside in a special account that my brother can access.

6. Give yourself a special treat which will divert your attention well away from this subject.

> *The thing you fear has no power. Your fear of it is what has the power.*
> **Oprah Winfrey, TV presenter**

Use imaginary mentors to psych you up

Don't be too sad. I went through some rough ones as well. One was here on this court last year . . . and I came back and won. You're an unbelievable guy . . . you are going to come back and win it. I really hope so.
Roger Federer, tennis champion (to his opponent, Andy Roddick)

Not all major winners in life are as generous and supportive as Roger Federer, but I do believe that although they may not get a chance to demonstrate this so publicly, very many others are. And although you may not be lucky enough to have such people at your side in real life right now, you can use your imagination to trick your emotional system into reacting as though you do; because your brain doesn't know the difference between real and imagined events, it will produce the same good feeling that hearing encouragement in real life from some of life's winners would bring.

Here's what to do:

* Compile a list of three to six people whom you admire for their persistence through times of difficulty. They could be people you know or famous figures (see the list of quotes below for inspiration). If possible, include one or two who have faced the same kind of challenge that you are facing. When I was facing a major financial

challenge, for example, I used my great-grandfather; he made and lost and regained many millions several times. I am sure if he had been there he would have given me perspective and some hope that my genetic inheritance might kick in! Similarly, when my daughter died, I recalled the faces of Isabel Allende, whose daughter also died, and Nelson Mandela, whose son died while he was on Robben Island. I have never been lucky enough to meet any of these courageous and generous-spirited people, but they have all, nevertheless, infused me with courage in my weaker moments.

* Whenever you feel like giving up or just want an extra push forward, close your eyes, take three slow, deep breaths, then recall the faces of your personal winners smiling encouragingly at you.

* Return their smile and, in your imagination, listen to each of them in turn giving you words of encouragement.

* Listen carefully to their words and keep smiling and breathing deeply as you do so. (The smiling and deep breathing will help you to receive the message and fix it in your memory.)

* Close your eyes and listen to your winners' encouragement whenever you need an instant boost of morale.

Words of encouragement

Here are some quotes from famous people who are/were known for their support of others. Choose one or two right now, close your eyes, relax your body by breathing deeply and listen in your mind to the encouragement that I am sure they would willingly give to you. You don't need to remember the words written here, just let your imagination work spontaneously. Later, you can compile a list of your own mentors to help you.

> *Making your mark on the world is hard. If it were easy, everybody would do it. But it's not. It takes patience, it takes commitment and it comes with plenty of failure along the way. The real test is not whether you avoid this failure, because you won't. It's whether you let it harden or shame you into inaction, or whether you learn from it; whether you choose to persevere.*
> **Barack Obama, the first black president of the USA**

> *We can do anything we want as long as we stick to it long enough.*
> **Helen Keller, who was left deaf and blind following an illness as a young child; she went on to become a world-famous speaker, author and campaigner for the disabled**

> *A champion is someone who gets up, even when he can't.*
> **Jack Dempsey – the boxer who battled through hardship and poverty to become a legendary world heavyweight champion**

> *I can stand out the war with any man.*
> **Florence Nightingale, who battled against her family, sexism, illness and the establishment to become a pioneering and legendary figure in the world of nursing**

QUICK FIX: Have a daily dip into a box full of buzz

This is a big favourite with my clients. The idea is that you fill a box with things that arouse good feelings in you instantly when you look at, touch, smell or hear them. Here are some ideas:

* Photos of loved ones
* Reminders of your goal and happier times that you are trying to reach
* Shells from a favourite beach
* Pebbles from a rippling brook in a favourite country spot
* A memorable perfume or aromatic oil
* CDs of evocative sounds, such as waves, birds or special songs and music
* Beautiful items of clothing or jewellery
* Small objects/carvings/sculptures

A variation on this idea is a good-memory box. When my daughter Laura died, we bought a beautiful chest into which we put items that brought back happy memories of her. You can also do something similar after a divorce. It can serve as a therapeutic closure exercise, but is also there for you to dip into whenever the 'bad' or overly sad memories surface and get in the way of you moving on.

The pain passes, but the beauty remains.
Pierre August Rodin, French sculptor, explaining why he still worked when his hands were twisted with arthritis

A hero is an ordinary individual who finds strength to persevere and endure in spite of overwhelming obstacles.
Christopher Reeve, the actor who played Superman, a few years after he was paralysed in an accident

 ## Battle with only one bad habit

When the going gets hard, you are at your most vulnerable to the destructive power of bad habits, and it is so easy at these times to convince yourself that you deserve a break from trying to break them. But what kind of treat is this in reality? You know, in your heart of hearts, that these kinds of habits take both your morale and self-esteem for a nose-dive.

Here are just a few examples of bad habits that can affect morale and slow you down.

* Discouraging self-talk

* Talking negatively about the future to others

* Not sticking to helpful routines or 'to-do' lists

* Watching too much TV

* Not eating well (skipping meals, eating fattening or junk food)

* Going to bed or getting up too late

* Letting good appearance habits slip

* Taking out your temper on people whom you need for support

* Drinking too much alcohol or caffeine

* Skipping energising physical exercise

* Not standing up for yourself when people disrespect you

* Trying to do too much in too little time

Getting the better of all such de-motivating habits is a guaranteed way to boost your morale. But while your life is already heavily pressurised, it makes sense to tackle only one bad habit at any given time.

Once you have chosen your habit, try to alter the way you look at it. View it as the dangerous 'enemy' that it actually is. This will make it easier to do battle with it. This is particularly important with the kinds of habit that give you instant pleasure and are therefore a major temptation. When you indulge in habits like these, you tend to feel 'mischievous', rather than truly 'bad'. You may:

* refer to them as 'naughty but nice'

* kid yourself that they are a necessary occasional treat – 'What's life about, if you can't enjoy yourself once in a while?'

* say, with a cheeky smile, 'I'll start tomorrow'.

Other people also often find pleasure in seducing you to commit these bad-habit 'sins'. ('Go on, be a devil . . . it's only this once!') And when others give in to their habits, don't we all feel slightly liberated from our own nagging consciences?

So the battle with a bad habit is often not just with yourself; it can be with your friends too. If this happens, a review of Section 9 will help you with this problem later; but for now, your first priority is to do what you can do. And the exercise below should help you.

You will need a pen and some paper as there are questions that you'll need to answer, and writing down your action points and finding someone to witness your commitment to them will increase your chances of winning the battle. You'll see that some of the questions suggest that a retreat from the battlefield is sometimes advisable. This is because you may need professional help, and it is much better to admit this at an early stage, rather than risk becoming even more demoralised and de-motivated.

> *Bad habits are easier to abandon today than tomorrow.*
> **Yiddish proverb**

Preparation for a habit-breaking battle

After choosing your habit, write down the answers to each of the following twelve questions:

1. What do you stand to gain if you win the war with this habit?

For example, you may feel more optimistic and self-confident and better able to move on at a faster rate.

2. *What are the conditions that will give your habit an advantage?*

This could be tiredness, experiencing a setback, receiving criticism from or being tempted by others.

3. *What do you stand to lose if you don't go to war with this habit?*

For example, you may become depressed, may not find another job/girlfriend/husband/house, etc.

4. *What is your motivating battle slogan?*

This could be something like, 'My will is stronger than this habit' or, 'I can conquer this'.

5. *What are your battle action goals?*

For example:

* 'My date for declaring war on this habit is . . . '

* 'The date for the first review of my progress is . . . '

* 'The date for the second review of my progress is . . . '

6. *How will you keep yourself motivated on a day-to-day basis?*

You could, for example, pin these notes up in the kitchen/office; reward yourself each evening with 10 minutes in the bath listening to music and sipping a long, cool drink.

7. *Who are your allies and what kind of support can they realistically give you?*

For example:

* 'John could help me review my progress.'

* 'Peter could remind me just before I start eating.'

* 'Both could help me celebrate if I make good progress.'

8. What are the warning signs that you might be losing ground in this battle?

For example, if you have given in more than twice in one week.

9. How will I know it is time to retreat and seek more help?

If, for example, your second 'battle review' (see above) has revealed that you have given in too many times (if possible, specify the number of failures in a month which, for you, would indicate that it is retreat time).

10. What will you do to obtain help as soon as you declare that you are retreating?

You might, for example, find more people to support you, enrol with a self-help group, see a counsellor or talk to your doctor.

11. How will you celebrate victory?

Take your 'allies' out for the night, for example.

12. Who can witness my signature on this declaration?

One of your 'allies' might do this.

Stop stress in its tracks

Tension is who you think you should be.
Relaxation is who you are.
Chinese proverb

Everyone now knows that stress is bad news; the research findings about its threat to health and life expectancy are always making headlines. And from your own life experience, you'll also know that it depresses your mood, disturbs relationships and is an arch-enemy of progress. So why does it so often get the better of us, even during the good times?

Stress builds stealthily, and in its earliest stages produces sensations that feel great and often make you perform more effectively. The initial adrenalin rush is energising – it lifts your mood and makes you feel more confident (if not arrogant!). And after this, there is no stopping or turning back; you are deaf to any feedback and too excited or busy for introspection.

The secret to stopping stress before it spirals down to burnout is to be alert to the symptoms that indicate a descent has just begun. There are slight negative changes that can be sensed and observed which, at this stage, have few – if any – serious consequences. Once past this critical phase, however, most people have to sink to a point where hurtful damage has set in before they will consider taking action.

Of course, during difficult times, you are even more vulnerable to stress. So it will pay big dividends to carry out a regular spot check on yourself, which you can do very quickly, using the checklist below.

The following early symptoms are common ones, some of which you will almost surely have experienced, while others you may not – much depends on your health, age and personality. You can also add a few of your own symptoms if you have identified any that are not listed. Show this checklist to your partner and/or friends too; they may be able to spot the signs earlier than you will.

Early warning stress signals

Physical

❑ Tension headaches – especially those which persist when you are 'at rest'

❑ Shallower breathing

❑ Less energy (perhaps taking the car or bus when it is easy to walk)

❑ Sweating more

❑ Unusual bowel movements

❑ Pins and needles when you stand or wake up

❑ Loss of libido (making the proverbial excuses)

❑ More frequent viruses

❑ Increase in allergic reactions

❑ Aching back or shoulders

❑ Restless legs and hands

- ❏ Cold hands and feet

- ❏ Increased PMT

- ❏ Congested sinuses

Emotional

- ❏ Increased anxiousness

- ❏ Moodiness for no apparent reason

- ❏ More pessimistic

- ❏ Not finding jokes so funny

- ❏ Persistent guilty thoughts

- ❏ Obsessive habits, such as wanting to check and recheck

- ❏ Feelings more easily hurt

- ❏ Apathy (saying, 'I don't mind' more often)

- ❏ Mistrustfulness (wondering about ulterior motives/ genuineness)

- ❏ Cynicism (making sneering remarks; negatively generalising)

- ❏ Overexcitement (having a one-track mind about an idea; being dismissive of alternatives)

- ❏ Depersonalisation (feeling at a distance from the world around you)

Mind/behaviour

- ❏ Concentration wandering more

- ❏ Inattentiveness (switching off when others are talking)

❏ Reclusiveness (not joining others at lunch; partying is less appealing)

❏ Increased alcohol intake

❏ Increased smoking

❏ Outbursts of irritation (making gratuitous biting remarks)

❏ Less careful about appearance

❏ Indecisiveness (letting others decide for you)

❏ More cautious (saying, 'I'm not sure' more often)

❏ Reluctance to delegate

❏ Making mountains out of molehills

❏ Going to bed later than usual

❏ Untidiness (being unable to find things)

❏ Disturbed sleep (restless; feeling less refreshed after sleep)

❏ Change in attitude to money (more spendthrift or opposite for no 'good' reason)

If you have ticked more than a couple of boxes, it's time to chill out a little. Don't just try to kid yourself that you can control the symptom/s – however good your intention, it is unlikely to last without making some lifestyle change. And Sections 1–3 of this book are filled with many ideas that are quick and easy to implement – so no excuses! Start experimenting now to find out which work best for you.

Check that your capabilities match your commitments

Thirty-nine-year-old Alice was divorced with two young children. Financially, she was reasonably comfortable, as her maintenance payments were supplemented by her part-time work as a book-jacket designer. But her family commitments were quite onerous: her father was suffering from Alzheimer's disease and her mother had had breast cancer and was still very weakened by the treatment. She planned to move to a house with a granny flat for her parents which would ease her child-care difficulties, while at the same time giving her mother, who loves her grandchildren, a positive focus and her father more attention. Although Alice had a circle of supportive friends she felt lonely and missed being part of a couple. She made a resolution to start actively seeking out opportunities to meet a new partner, but six months on, she felt that she was getting nowhere and her morale was at a very low ebb.

One of the first tasks that Alice needed to tackle was to look at how she could cut down on her commitments. It was obvious that she could not manage them in her current state and that things could therefore only get worse for her unless and until she took action.

Over-commitment is one of the most common causes of low morale. A key task for the manager of a successful organisation is to ensure constantly that there is a manage-able balance between the capabilities of each member of staff and the commitments that they are expected to meet. This is the exact principle that Alice had to apply to herself in this situation.

Assess the match between your capabilities and commitments

In the table below, you'll see that I have identified seven types of capability that are usually needed to handle and keep people going during difficult times (you can change or add to these, if there are others that are more relevant to your situation). To illustrate how this exercise works, I've reproduced Alice's assessment of the match between her own capabilities and commitments. The ticks indicate an OK level of capability in that commitment area.

Capabilities	*Commitments*				
	Search for new partner	House move	Childcare	Working life	Mum and Dad support
Physical capacities	✓		✓	✓	✓
Emotional reserves		✓		✓	
Thinking functions	✓		✓		✓
Confidence levels				✓	✓
Financial and material resources	✓	✓	✓	✓	✓
Skills/ knowledge levels			✓	✓	✓
Supply of support	✓	✓	✓	✓	

If your assessment reveals an imbalance, you will need to cut down on your commitments, delegate aspects of them or improve your capability. Alice's notes (below) will give you an idea of how this can be done.

Alice's action notes

1. Should postpone plans to move house.

2. To boost me emotionally I need to spend more quality time with Fiona [her best friend] – perhaps we could go on weekend retreat together when ex- comes over from the States in the summer.

3. Not thinking very creatively at work but can coast OK for a while longer. Break should help.

4. Must give myself an urgent confidence boost (Section 2 of this book).

5. Ring social worker at the hospital next week and see if I can get home nursing support for Mum and Dad.

6. Perhaps can start to find out more about dating agencies, even though my capabilities are way too low to start yet.

> *I am only one*
> *But still I am one*
> *I cannot do everything*
> *But I can do something*
> **Edward Everett Hale, author and statesman**

QUICK FIX: Permit pauses in your progress

Moving on from hard times rarely goes forward consistently. There will be setbacks and periods when nothing appears to be happening. You need to accept this and plan ahead as to how you will use any such 'waiting' time constructively.

Being self-employed, I've had to learn how to do this. I keep certain administrative office work and house-maintenance tasks for such low-activity periods. Also, on birthdays and at Christmas, my husband often gives me a present of a day in a spa. These will be filed away and used during one of the fallow periods in my work schedule. Another favourite filler activity of mine is to do some catching up with friends.

Why not apply the same principle to the dips in your momentum? Think of positive tasks you could do should you encounter a setback or have to wait around for finance or someone to do something before you can step forward again. Then, instead of feeling fed up, you will find yourself saying, 'Great – this gives me a chance to catch up on/learn/finish/start . . .'

Surprise yourself with your rewards for effort

To maintain your momentum, it is very important to focus on rewarding your good efforts rather than waiting until success arrives. If you are having a very difficult time with a tough challenge, this is especially important. It may be a long time before you will feel truly satisfied that you have recovered or moved on.

If you've ever trained a dog, you'll know how important it is to vary the rewards you give them. This is why their treats are usually sold in variety packs. Every time you dip your hand into the pack neither you nor your dog knows what will be brought out. And while, of course, there may be some major differences between you and dogs, in this respect you are predictably the same! You can expect a much better performance from yourself if you randomly rotate your rewards. The surprise element is exciting, pleasurable and so much more satisfying.

It will pay you to prepare some rewards so that you can give them to yourself fairly quickly after you have made a good effort. Here are two suggestions:

* Buy yourself a number of small gifts, and wrap them in bubble wrap to disguise their shape before you cover them with paper. Keep these in a drawer or box, then close your eyes and take a dip into the pile whenever you deserve a treat.

* Take some plain cards and write out a treat on each one, such as:

  • dinner at a certain restaurant

  • a CD or special book that you would like

  • a new accessory

  • an outing or weekend break

  • quality time with a certain person.

* Pop these cards in a clear plastic envelope and keep it in your handbag or briefcase. Then, when you've had a success or taken a step forward in your recovery (however small), shuffle your cards, pick one out at random and give yourself that treat.

QUICK FIX: Hum yourself happy

This is a great, simple tip from Dr Daniel G. Amen, author of *Change Your Brain, Change Your Life.* Dr Amen, a psychiatrist and neuroscientist (which means that his wisdom is based on seeing for himself how the brain reacts when people do certain things, as well as his considerable clinical experience), says that humming enhances both mood and memory.

So you can lift your spirits and tune your mind at the same time. Dr Amen suggests that we consciously focus on humming from time to time during the day. But don't wait until the going gets any tougher; give your morale and momentum an easy boost by starting a happy hum right now!

Power yourself into action with goals

First say to yourself what you would be; and then do what you have to do.

Epictetus, Greek philosopher

Epictetus was born into slavery and suffered many setbacks in his life (including physical disability and exile), yet he became one of mankind's most influential philosophers. The wisdom that he imparted concerning personal power is as relevant today for anyone who is encountering tough times as it ever was.

Epictetus believed that the key to recovery is to use your personal power effectively. So rather than focusing on those aspects of what has happened to you that were, or are, beyond your control, you should deal with something that is within your power to change – namely, yourself and your attitudes. So now is the time to give your momentum a real push forward by making some resolutions to use your personal power in the most effective ways that you can. Goal-setting is crucial for this, but only if it is done well.

First, you must have a long-term dream that is challenging enough to inspire you, but realistic enough to ensure that you have a fair chance of realising it. Next, you need a series of step-by-step objectives with deadlines to give you a sense of achievement and an opportunity for some well-deserved rewards along the way. The following exercise will help you to put this theory into action and to firm up your commitment to keeping your morale as high as it possibly can be in difficult times.

Your goal-setting plan of action

Fill in the blank spaces in the statements below. Try to do this exercise now or at least by the end of the day or tomorrow, at the latest. You can always write in pencil and make changes later if necessary, but you will get an instant boost from doing some goal-setting immediately.

1. In five years' time I intend to be able to look back at this period and feel _____. (For example, 'a sense of achievement', 'inner peace', 'in control', etc.)

2. In five years' time I intend to _____. (For example, 'be doing more work that satisfies me', 'have established a support group to help others in the same situation', 'be living happily with a new partner', etc.)

3. By the end of next year I will have _____. (For example, 'conquered my fear', 'be driving again', 'paid off the loan from my mother', etc.)

4. In six months' time I will have _____. (For example, 'signed up with a dating agency if I haven't met anyone', 'chosen a couple of alternative career options', etc.)

5. In one month's time, I will have _____. (For example, 'seen a debt-management consultant', 'improved my sleep regime', etc.)

6. The three tips in this book that I will reread and use immediately to give me the morale boost I need are:

* _____

* _____

* _____

Difficulties are things that show a person what they are ... It's not what happens to you, but how you react to it that matters.
Epictetus

A Final Word

As you must have gathered from reading this book, my own life has been peppered with all manner of setbacks. However, I know that there are many other difficulties that I could have faced and there may be even more just around the corner.

And you too may be aware – and fearful – of the 'unknown'. Perhaps you are even thinking along these lines right now, and feeling sceptical about the future, despite having read through this collection of tips. But I hope that you will soon start to put many of them into action in earnest, because when you do, you will start to feel differently. Then, in the future, should your self-confidence and trust in the world be knocked back again, you will find that the skills you have acquired for recovering your psychological power will automatically flip back into the forefront of your mind.

Most importantly, this will be true even when you cannot improve your physical or material circumstances. It was only when this happened to me personally – when my daughter Laura was killed – that I believed this could really be so. During this period, I used to repeat the following Chinese proverb to myself: 'You cannot prevent the birds of *sadness* from flying over your head, but you can prevent them from nesting in your hair.' I have taken the liberty of highlighting the word 'sadness' here because I have found that it can be replaced with other emotions that affect morale negatively during difficult times (such as guilt, jealousy or anger), so that the proverb's wisdom can be applied in many situations.

Finally, perhaps once you are feeling stronger in yourself, you will pass on your new knowledge and insight to anyone else who may be struggling to stay positive through problem situations. Not only will this give them much-needed comfort and encouragement, it will also strengthen your own morale further still.

So, good luck – and I hope that armed with your 101 morale boosters, you'll find your recovery is quicker than you'd ever dreamed possible.

Resources

Further Reading

Dr Daniel G. Amen, *Change Your Brain, Change Your Life* (Piatkus, 2009)

Daniel Gilbert, *Stumbling on Happiness* (Harper Perennial, 2007)

Gael Lindenfield, *The Emotional Healing Strategy* (Penguin, 2008)

Gael Lindenfield, *Managing Anger* (HarperCollins, 1993)

Gael Lindenfield and Stuart Lindenfield, *Confident Networking for Career Success and Satisfaction* (Piatkus, 2005)

Organisations and individuals mentioned in this book

Anxiety UK
Zion CRC
339 Stretford Road
Hulme, Manchester M15 4ZY
Tel: 0161 227 9898
Tel/fax: 08444 775 774

Email: info@anxietyuk.org.uk
Website: www.anxietyuk.org.uk

Brain Gym UK
Tel: 0845 539 0312
Website: www.braingym.org.uk

FairBanking
A summary of the work and research of this charity dedicated to the wellbeing of bank customers can be found on their website: www.fairbanking.org.uk

Friends of the Earth
26–8 Underwood Street
London N1 7JQ
Tel: 020 7490 1555
Contact by email via this website: www.foe.co.uk

Sandra Nathan (Emotional Freedom Technique)
Contact Sandra by email via this website:
www.freeyourself-eft.com

The Red Hat Society
Information and contact details are on this website:
www.britishredhatters.ik.com

Thrive

The charity that uses gardening
to change lives.
The Geoffrey Udall Centre
Beech Hill
Reading RG7 2AT
Tel: 0118 988 5688
Contact by email via this website:
www.thrive.org.uk

Other useful UK-based organisations

Most of these organisations could
also recommend additional books
to read and appropriate services:

The Mental Health Foundation

A leading UK charity that
provides information, carries out
research, campaigns and works
to improve services for anyone
affected by mental-health
problems, regardless of age
or circumstances.
9th Floor
Sea Containers House
20 Upper Ground
London SE1 9QB
Email:webteam@mhf.org.uk
Website: www.mentalhealth.org.uk

Mind

A leading charity which
campaigns and provides services
for people with mental-health
problems.
15–19 Broadway
Stratford
London E15 4BQ
Tel.: 020 8519 2122
Fax: 020 8522 1725
Email: contact@mind.org.uk
Website: www.mind.org.uk

YoungMinds

Charity committed to improving
the emotional wellbeing of
children and young people.
48–50 St John Street
London
EC1M 4DG
Tel: 020 7336 8445
Website: www.youngminds.org.uk

Gael Lindenfield

For information on Gael's
other books and services and
to contact her, please visit her
website:
www.gaellindenfield.com

Useful organisations in Australia and New Zealand

The Mental Health Foundation of Australia

270 Church Street
Richmond
Vic 3121
Tel: +61 3 9427 0407
Fax: +61 3 9427 1294
Website: www.mhfa.org.au

SANE Australia

A national charity that campaigns to help people affected by mental illness. It also runs a helpline.
PO Box 226
South Melbourne
Victoria
Australia
3205
Tel: +61 3 9682 5933
Fax: +61 3 9682 5944
Email: info@sane.org
Website: www.sane.org

The Mental Health Foundation of New Zealand

81 New North Road
Eden Terrace
Auckland
Tel: (09) 300 7010
Fax: (09) 300 7020
Website: www.mentalhealth.org

Index